T0086375

# Personalizing the Bible

# PERSONALIZING THE BIBLE

## BY MY BIRTHDAY VERSES

HE Bramble

**PERSONALIZING THE BIBLE**
**BY MY BIRTHDAY VERSES**

iUniverse books may be ordered through booksellers or by contacting:

iUniverse
1663 Liberty Drive
Bloomington, IN 47403
www.iuniverse.com
844-349-9409

All Scripture quotations not otherwise designated are from
the King James Version (KJV) of the Bible.

Permission to quote from the following additional copyrighted
versions of the Bible is acknowledged with appreciation:

The Holy Bible, English Standard Version (ESV®). Text Edition: 2016. Copyright ©2001 by Crossway Bibles, a publishing ministry of Good News Publishers.

The Message (MSG). Copyright © 1993, 2002, 2018 by Eugene H. Peterson.

Holy Bible, New International Version®, (NIV®). Copyright ©1973, 1978, 1984, 2011 biblical, Inc.®Used by permission. All rights reserved worldwide.

New American Standard Bible(NASB). Copyright © 1960, 1962, 1963, 1968, 1971, 1972, 1973, 1975, 1977, 1995 by The Lockean Foundation

ISBN: 978-1-6632-2344-9 (sc)
ISBN: 978-1-6632-2349-4 (e)

Print information available on the last page.

iUniverse rev. date: 04/26/2022

# CONTENTS

# About the Author
# My cover page story

I am a 76 year old that has a brand new vocation in life in writing this book. I was born in Maryland on the Eastern shore side of the state on a farm. I was nearsighted which caused problems in school. At the age of 25, married and with two kids felt the need for more schooling. You see I was a graduate and could not spell the word (graduate). I got the words (this) and (that) mixed up, (was) and (were) confusing to me. O yes! I needed more schooling alright, so I chose a bible school to go to. I did not realize it then but God had a plan to not only to get my much needed schooling, but with a bible based knowledge of His word also. It took me five more years to get my bible degree and a BA degree in education. These seventy six years of my life have many twists and turns, but I through the leading and guidance of the Lord Jesus and the blessed holy Spirit I made it, With my stroke and my computer at my fingertips, God has allowed me to put down on paper the things that have been stored up in my heart. I hope this book "personalizing the bible is one of many. I have one called "3 levels and 7 positions."

will be my next one. I live here in Helen Georgia with my wife and together 6 children and 13 grandchildren 7 great-grandchildren, all living in three states, Georgia, North and South Carolina and one in France with her husband and her four. My preacher, the pastor of the church I attended in my bible school days, "said he hoped to die with hundreds of unfulfilled dreams. Never give up. As long as God gives me breath, I will move forward also.

Napoleon Hill says:

**Success requires no explanation; failures must be doctored with alibis.**

The surest way to achieve acceptance in any organization or in any line of work is to be successful. Unfortunately, life doesn't work that way. No matter how carefully you study a subject, no matter how rationally you make decisions, no matter how well prepared you are, you will occasionally make mistakes. Human beings always do. The important thing is to realize that temporary setbacks are not permanent failures. Successful people recognize that we all experience temporary setbacks that require us to reevaluate our performance and take corrective action to achieve success. They know that adversity is never permanent

# A DEDICATION PAGE

I want to dedicate this book to my wife, the love of my life. Her patience, understanding and love has been a big help to me as I spend long hours at my computer in my office at home, without interruptions.

We met in Lavonia Georgia, the halfway point between Greenville SC and Helen Ga. on August 12,2014, after getting acquainted online, six months later we got married on Valentine's day, it fell on Saturday of that year, 2015. I tell people that I married my sweetheart on valentines' day. The website we used was a famous dating service. They line us up by our personality traits,

She is an Sanguine, an introvert, a people-Oriented and an optimist. I am a Choleric, an Extrovert and task-Oriented. We have on our computer the ups and downs of both of the Sanguine and a choleric traits together in marriage with our personality traits also with Dr. Gary Chapman's book the five love Language for married couples. We get along great. Now her love language is "word of encouragement, and gifts of service. She likes me fixing the coffee for her in the mornings. She tells everyone that I am a good christian husband because "Hebrews" the coffee. Now there was a bit of challenge with our love languages, because mine was the same, so I am learning to change mine to meet up with hers.. Can I say here that she is a different person from me and that is what God intended it to be. She is wired emotionally and I am wired mentally. She is multi-tasted and I am single tasted. She is of the motherly type and I am in the leadership role, the list goes on and on, we have all the years of marriage to figure that out.

I say of her that she is a pm person, you can take the AM out of her day and she will be just fine. I am an AM person, I was raised on a farm and milked cows, need I say more.

I asked her to marry me so on my birthday and gave her an engagement ring. I tell people, I did that so I would not forget the date. No! God worked out the plans for us. Now that is not saying we are not without trials and setbacks, every couple has them; Job tells us in his book in the bible, that "life is few days and full of troubles".

She was married twice before, same as I, but hers was two deaths, one lasted fifty years and produced three children, two girls and one boy, one lasted two years, he died from Cancer, I had two failed marriages, so there is a big amen to my wife. Taking a big change on me. It was a little challenging for me for the first two years however with the longevity of her second husband. I have three children: two girls and one boy, both boys are in the middle.


## A dedication to my stroke

I know you are saying right now, Harry, you are crazy, being thankful for your stroke. It was a driving force for my stick-ability to stay with writing this book, and hope others books will follow. I am Seventy six and just getting started.

A mini-stroke is a temporary blockage in the body,

mine was in the top of my head in the brain area, left side, it temporarily intruded my speech, it got to my right side, therefore it caused problems with my balance. For that, I have the stick-ability to stay with my writing/typing of this book. I have dozens of uncompleted jobs. I will start to read a book and go to the next one before I have finished the one that I have been reating. That's how choleric temperament is. Now back to my stroke, because of it, I have a lot of balance issues and so setting here at my computer, I can type as though nothing is wrong. God has given me the go power to type without problems..

Let me quote a couple of bible verses for you to read that will back up from scripture what I am trying to say:

I Corinthians 10:13 **"There hath no temptation taken you but such as is common to man: but God is faithful, who will not suffer you to be tempted above that ye are able; but will with the temptation also make a way to escape, that ye may be able to bear it."** (KJV)

Colossians 1:24 **"Who now rejoice in my sufferings for you, and fill up that which is behind of the afflictions of Christ in my flesh for his body's sake, which is the church."** (KJV)

Philippians 1:12 **"But I would ye should understand, brethren, that the things which happened unto me have fallen out rather unto the furtherance of the gospel"** (KJV)

By me writing this book will give you as the reader a jump start claiming the bible in your life more. By having your birthday verses, you will make the bible part of you. An edge up on life itself, Mind is September 16, September is the ninth month and so I use the ninth chapter of each book of the bible and verse 16 of that chapter.

# Acknowledgment

As I type this book I am learning real fast that it takes a team of people to put my book together: I want to thank Johnathan Wright for type sitting, Clay Dean my Gideon buddy who kept my computer skills up to par, Garrison Baker another of my Gideon buddies that wrote the very famous book "in the shadows of Mount Yonah, Yonah is a famous landmark, a mountain peak in white county Georgia. Along with the famous other attractions in White County such as the Swiss town of Helen, with its Alpine buildings, home of the cabbage patch dolls, and a slew of winneys, many mountainous trails to hike on. David Britnell, another Gideon friend who helped with my spelling and structuring of my sentences. Guy Michaels on my proofreading and Kimberly Carter a church friend.

Just a word about the Gideon s international, they are an 110 year group that passes out the word of God to corporate America. We have four forms of God. God the father and God the Son and God the blessed Holy Spirit, and God the word. Look at John 1:1-2 & 14

**In the beginning was the Word, and the Word was with God, and the <u>Word was God.</u>**

**The same was in the beginning with God.** 14 **And the**

**Word was made flesh,** (Jesus) **and dwelt among us,** (and we beheld his glory, the glory as of the only begotten of the Father,) full of grace and truth. (KJV This is what He had in mind from the start, We behold His Glory. Heaven is an unending place of glory, because He is there.

**I John 1:1 "That which was from the beginning, which we have heard, which we have seen with our eyes, which we have looked at and our hands have touched—** (this alone prioritize the word of God) **this we proclaim concerning the Word of life."** (KJV) Did you realize that when you are handling the word of God, you are handing out Jesus? This alone makes it personal to us.

# INTRODUCTION

It was a Saturday morning in Greenville SC, just a good day in the Spring, Sun was shining and the birds were singing, cars with its passages were buzzing the highways, so seemed to be a normal June day, however a bit of war was raging inside my head. I was having a severe panic attack. Every demon in hell seems to be inside me. After 34 years of marriage, she walked out on me. As it turned out to be a turning point in life, at the age of fifty three I was about to tread new waters of life. I told my buddy, Rick, about it and he reorganized it immediately. This was right up his alley of study, in the classroom they studied cases like this one that I was having. When we go through a panic attack is when we allow the pressure around us to come inward! We allow Satan to do his dirty work inside our hearts. Now Rick was getting his master's degree in Counseling from Masters college, Dr. John McAuthor's college in California. He needed a case study on marriage counseling and I needed help with what I was going through, it was God's perfect timing.

Now back to Saturday morning with this strange chain of events, I was hyperventilating, I was in a bad way emotionally. I was born on a Saturday afternoon. How cool is that, I drew my first breath of life on Saturday and I was in a bad way emotional on Saturday. I have had my extreme ups and downs on Saturdays, it seems.

I was at that point of suicidal and a danger to myself, I wanted out of my body and out real fast. I told Rick that if I had a gun, I believe I would have used it. He told me to go home and do as Hezekiah did and spread it out before the Lord, and that is what I did

II Kings 19:1&14 **"And it came to pass, when king Hezekiah heard it, that he rent his clothes, and covered himself with sackcloth, and went into the house of the Lord.** (KJV)

II Kings 19:14 **"And Hezekiah received the letter of the hand of the messengers, and read it: and Hezekiah went up into the house of the Lord, and spread it before the Lord."** (KJV)

That act has changed my life up to the present and I feel like it will be smoother sailing to the end of this life. When A problem arises, just spread it out before Him and tell Him about it. He already knows about it, just waiting for us to come to Him with the problem.

Napoleon Hill quotes: **Most illness begins with a negative mind.**

Andrew Carnegie says *"Most of the important things in this world have been accomplished by people who have kept on trying when there seemed to be no hope at all."*

Before I leave this section, let me do some comparison with some analogies. The dictionary has it as a comparison between two things. I like to compare it with God and us, therefore we can understand it and to personalize the bible better. I have already used the males and the females in my dedication to my wife. Now let us look at Christ and we as humans, Let take God and a dog, why I used this is because of the spelling. God is dog spelled backwards and vice versa, God wants us to see man and his dog and the difference, Just as the dog is inferior to man in action, intellectually and emotionally, so are men in this degree with God. By comparing the two, we get the bigger picture of God and us as humans. We can relate and therefore personalize His word character to our lives.

When I went on a missionary trip to Trinidad, I saw the whole island in one glance with no problem as long as I was up high above the island (The island is big as New Jersey) but as I got closer the island became bigger. Like the analogy of a crochet picture: we as humans can see just the bottom of the picture with strings hanging down everywhere, a real mess it looks to us. But God sees the top of the picture of a basket of beautiful flowers with a pure blue sky above and the bright sun shining through the cottoney clouds on the green wet grass just after the rain.

Let me give you another analogy: we get our DNA from our mothers and fathers. Jesus has no earthly father, so his Dna has partly Heaven, for the Holy Spirit was His father, Luke 1:35 **And the angel answered and said unto her, The Holy Ghost shall come upon thee, and the power of the Highest shall overshadow thee: therefore also that holy thing which shall be born of thee shall be called the Son of God.** (KJV)

Because of His heavenly DNA from His father, He can do things that we can not do. Like He knows what is in the heart of man John 2:24-25 **But Jesus did not commit himself unto them, because he knew all men,** 25 **And**

**needed not that any should testify of man: for he knew what was in man.** (KJV) Mattews 9:4 **"And Jesus knowing their thoughts said, Wherefore think ye evil in your hearts?** (KJV) Matthews 12:25 **"And Jesus knew their thoughts, and said unto them, Every kingdom divided against itself is brought to desolation; and every city or house divided against itself shall not stand.** (KJV)

Luke 9:47-48 **"And Jesus, perceiving the thought of their heart, took a child, and set him by him, 48 And said unto them, Whosoever shall receive this child in my name receiveth me: and whosoever shall receive me receiveth him that sent me: for he that is least shall be great.** (KJV)

**I John 3:20 "For if our heart condemns us, God is greater than our heart, and knoweth all things.** (KJV)

Psalms 44:21 **"I Shall not God search this out for He knoweth the secrets of the heart."** (KJV) (and we think we can out smart God when He knows every corner of our heart, every pet habits we have, the secret is not on God's side but our side. You see we do not know our own heart. Jeremiah 17:9 **"The heart is deceitful above all things, and desperately wicked: who can know it?** (KJV) There you have seven verses where God knows. We could go on and on with just that subject alone. This is how rich the bible is to us, if we will let it be in our lives, but We are the stopping force, not God. God knows who will get saved and who will not yield to salvation in Christ. This is where my faith comes in, this is too high for Bramble to understand. I do not want to understand, only believe that God has complete control and knows what He is doing. God by His Spirit has given us one fruit but nine avenues that fruit will develop in us and from us. I will cover in detail in the third section of this book.

God gave me this ideal of personalizing my birthday verses about four years ago, and it has worked so well that I thought I would pass it along with my blessings. It has put more life into the Bible for me. The thirty one verses have been a huge blessing for me and have carved out a personality I didn't know I had but was always there. My birthdays so fit my Bible reading schedule that I have appropriated one verse per day, starting with Genesis 9:16 as the first day to Revelation 9:16 as the thirty first day. This book is a "Cliffs-notes" to my longer book coming out later, titled *Three Levels and Seven Positions. Death, my other book I am working on. Death is real as we think of it as real. This too is another book title that I will attempt to write about. Death, a false enemy that we got caught up into, like George Bernard Shaw wrote, "The statistics on death are quite impressive. One out of one people die." The bible has a lot to say about death. So personalizing the bible gives you the upper hand on the subject of death. Knowledge gives power and boldness. Death then to us becomes fearless and powerless. Death is a mode of transportation from this world to the next. From this body of sinful flesh to a everlasting glorified body,*

*Dr. Billy Graham's father-in-law Dr. L. Nelson Bell wrote "Only those who are prepared to die are really prepared to live." The uncertainty is not the dying, it's the preparation.*

The Psalmist says in 34:8 "**to taste and see**" (KJV) (Taste here is to perceive) The glorified bodies in heaven do` not eat like we eat, they perceive or enjoy. Other renderings for taste is perception, (in the mouth, like french kissing),

Jesus used it in the gospels as palpitate, (palpitation of

the heart) In John chapter 6 Jesus was not saying to taste His flesh but to enjoy it from the heart. They misunderstood Him and we read in verse 66 "many went back and walked with Him no more" Now we have the first time that 666 is used and it is not in a good sense. John 6:66 We simply do not savor the taste of Jesus's life and what He has done for us on the cross of Calvary for our sins.. Like the word love, there are at least seven words for love in the Greek language and in our English language we have only one word. We try to make the bible that was written in Hebrew and Greek to fit our western civilian today. This creates a lot of versions of the bible and many many denominations in our christian worship. Satan loves it because it carries out his plan of divide and conquer. He is a liar and the father of all lies

Twenty-two books of the Old Testament have chapter 9 verse 16 in them and nine in the New Testament, a total of thirty-one

So if you were born on January the 6th, that would be the first chapter of each book of the bible and verse 6, which would be all 66 books, now if your birthday is December the 31, This would be the twelfth chapter and 31st verse of that chapter. Your birthday verses would be not many. Your first birthday verse would be in Exodus 12:31 **"And he** (Pharaoh: king of Egypt) **called Moses and Aaron by night, and said Rise and get you forth from among my people, both ye and the children of Israel; and go, serve the Lord as ye have said,"** (KJV) To me this verse is a challenge, to see what Moses and Aaron would do, Pharaoh had no intentions of letting the children of Israel go.

Now back to my birthday verses, I cannot rule out the mind-over-matter theory. We frequently see things in a way that they will fit us and our current lifestyle. I try to be aware of this in reading each of my birthday verses and go with the flow, letting things fall as they may. I try taking myself completely out of the picture, letting go and letting God do His work in my Life..

Romans 7:24 says, **O wretched man that I am! who shall deliver me from the body of this death?** (KJV) Here Paul is finishing up his personal testimony. The previous verses in this chapter, verses 14–24, are most valuable. This text is a tongue-twister—but so true of our trying to serve the Lord:

> **For we know that the law is spiritual: but I am carnal, sold under sin. For that which I do I allow not: for what I would, that do I not; but what I hate, that do I. If then I do that which I would not, I consent unto the law that it is good. Now then it is no more I that do it, but sin that dweller in me. For I know that in me** (that is, in my flesh,) **dweller no good thing: for to will is present with me; but how to perform that which is good I find not. For the good that I would I do not: but the evil which I would not, that I do. Now if I do that I would not, it is no more I that do it, but sin that dweller in me. I find then a law, that, when I would do good, evil is present with me. For I delight in the law of God after the inward man: But I see another law in my members, warring against the law of my mind, and bringing me into captivity to the law of sin which is in my members. O wretched man that I**

**am! Who shall deliver me from the body of this death?** (KJV)

David also says in Psalm 55:3-4" **The wicked are estranged from the womb: they go astray as soon as they be born, speaking lies.** (We need a Savior to lead us, we are all wicked and you and I <u>must</u> be born again) 4 **Their poison is like the poison of a serpent:** (this was me before I got saved) **they are like the deaf adder that stoppeth her ear;"** (KJV) Before I was saved, refused hearing the word of God, it was offensive to me, it made no sense. I was twenty years old at that time and accountable for my sins. Now I cannot leave this section without saying that God in His infinite wisdom has all the babies born before accountability covered. This could be up to 8 years with some babies. Now if they have any mental issues going on, they are automatically covered while in that state, if that is for life. Only God knows this, He only can see the heart. Jeremiah says **"The heart is deceitful above all things, and desperately wicked: who can know it?"** (KJV)

I already have my last name mentioned in the Bible: **Then said all the trees unto the *bramble*, Come thou, and reign over us. And the *bramble* said unto the trees, If in truth ye anoint me king over you, then come and put your trust in my shadow: and if not, let fire come out of the *bramble*, and devour the cedars of Lebanon** Judges 9:14–15. **And thorns shall come up in her palaces, nettles and *brambles* in the fortresses thereof: and it shall be an habitation of dragons, and a court for owls** (KJV) Isaiah 34:13. This verse includes my family. Bramble is a thorn (bush). That is why they called me in school

"Bramble Bush." And Luke 6:44 Jesus acknowledged my name: **Every tree known by his own fruit. For of thorns men do not gather figs, nor of a _bramble_ bush gather they grapes**.(KJV)

This was a parable of leadership. Verse 39 of the same chapter. **And He** (Jesus) **spake a parable unto them,** (KJV) (The scribes and the Pharisees, v.7) Bramble or Brambles are mentioned five times in the King James Version of the Bible.

Five stands for grace. I like to remember that I have the grace of God living in me.

G-God is my Savior

R-Redeemer of my soul

A-He is my Authority

C-Christ is all and all in my life

E-the Eternal One

The Psalmist tells us that we were born into sin: **Behold, I was shape in iniquity; and in sin did my mother conceive me** (Psalm 51:5 KJV). Paul sees this force threatening to take over his body and in Ephesians 6:11–18 encourages us to put on the whole armor of God. I want to personalize the Bible to help me when the evil forces come at me.

These verses in Judges, Isaiah and Luke include my family, Bramble is a thorn bush. That is why they called me in school "Bramble Bush or Bramble briers, they met no harm but it cost me some anxiety issues in life. Be sensitive in your dealings with your talk with and about other people.

I got Saved fifty five years ago in a Thompson street apartment in Hurlock, Maryland, It was one of the Thursdays in November of 1965. Why I remembered Thursday was the next night my buddy Jimmy and I went out to play pool on Friday nights,

9

My name is Harry Bramble, Our names hold a meaning, what is yours. So far I can't brag on my name, or can I? I know that God is still working on me. Yes! Bramble means ruler and authority-"the power and the right to give orders, make decisions, and enforce obedience." Now, that's my problem. With this in mind, out of the 31,102 verses in the King James bible, I had to pick John 3:30 "**He must increase and I must decrease." (KJV)** God has a sense of humor. He knows how to get my attention.

Why are frogs so happy? Answer: because they eat whatever bugs them.

Here's another one "I know only 25 letters of the English alphabet, I don't know "Y"

You see a little humor goes a long way for your mental and emotional conditions. If we can only see the big picture of what God is doing to us and for us, it would make you laugh with excitement. God has our best at heart. In the proverbs 17:22 **"A merry heart doeth good like a medicine: but a broken spirit drieth the bones."** (You have (no morrow (liquid) in dried bones). Talking about our bones acken, you could not stand it without liquid in your bones, especially in the joint areas.

Harry, my first name, comes from Harold, which means "ruler," so we have a ruler in *Harry* and a dictatorship in *bramble*. Thank God for my middle name, Edward, which means "wealth" and "guard." All three stand for ruling of some sort. But Edward—let's take the wealth side. I have enjoyed business and accounting since I was a young boy. In my book *Three Levels and Seven Positions,* which is coming out soon, I tell of my business experience, which started with the making of pot holders at age six. My dad gave me five acres of land when I was sixteen, and at the age of 40 I had rental houses for the past twenty-five years in Greenville, South Carolina. I got my start in the business world when my younger sister and I would play Monopoly for hours on end, a board game based on real-life business. I can still tell you all the properties, the values of each, and the cost of the houses and hotels in this old game. I understand now they have changed the values. When I was not working on the farm, usually on rainy days, we would play Monopoly or I would make up math problems usually related to the farm, working on made up math problems for hours. I enjoy working with figures. My last verse of the bible that has 9:16 is in Revelations and it deals with numbers. Right on Jesus! He knows me. As for the "guard" side of Edward, I'm very aware of the need to guard my testimony every minute of every day. I do not want anyone to fall because of me. Matthew 5:16 "**Let your light so shine before men, that they may see your good works, and glorify your Father which is in heaven.** (KJV)

I enjoy money just like any other person does, but I enjoy it when I get it by the sweat of my brow, by the toil of my hands. O the satisfaction you get doing things the right way. You can sleep better at night, your food tastes better, your body operates smoother. You can smile at your self pride and dance for the fullest of life that you have.

Personalizing the Bible is much like the time when my younger sister, Faye, and I were small and our parents would take us on a Sunday afternoon drive. We would get lost sometimes, or so Faye and I thought. We told Daddy to turn onto this road or that one, and he would do it. We would stop at a country store and buy a loaf of bread, some lunch meat, and usually mustard with which to make sandwiches and then go to a remote place to eat our lunch. Remote spots are hard to find now, with houses popping up everywhere. Daddy and mom did that just for us. Looking back now, I knew we were making wonderful memories. These Sunday afternoon drives were personal for my younger sister and I. Dad, Mom, and my two brothers are gone now, and the life of my older sister, Mary Agnes' ("Sis") life was cut short in a car accident. Time moves on.

Death is part of life and we just have to deal with it. These thirty one verses are my birthday verses, and I lay claim to the other thirty thousand verses in the Bible, which is my road map. My birthday verses are an everlasting lesson for me. I'm finding out about myself as I write this book. I will give you an example, Romans 9:16 "**so then it is not of him that willeth, nor of him that runner, but of God that sheathe mercy.**" I am willing to do and I am running to do, but it is of His mercy. I just have to be willing to be used. If that means walking, or running. It is all about Him, it's not about me. My personality is Choleric, an extrovert, task-oriented and a decision-maker. There are 9 temperaments, 9 fruits of the Spirit, and 5 love languages and four personality traits. So I am a reformer in my temperament, for one and Love is the first fruit of the Spirit. My second temperament is the investigator and the fruit of the Spirit is kindness. My third tenement is the challenger and the fruit of the Spirit for that is gentleness. My love language is "words of affirmation". Sorry to say I did not receive it growing up and I feel like I was a failure in it with my first wife and the children. I feel like mom and day love me, but they just did not know how to show it. The bible has a lot to say about confidence which at the start of my life, I had very little of. We will cover more on confidence in my daily bible reading in the third section of this book. I have a whole section in my future book on confidence. Satan does not want God's people to have confidence. **Psalm 118:8-9 "It is better to trust in the Lord than to put confidence** (trust) **in man. 9 It is better to trust in the Lord than to put confidence in princes."** (KJV)

**II Timothy 1:12 "For the which cause I also suffer these things: nevertheless I am not ashamed:**(I have confidence) **for I know whom I have believed, and am persuaded that he is able to keep that which I have committed unto him against that day. (KJV)**

God comes to us in four forms: the Father, the Son, the Holy Spirit, and the word. John 1:1-2 & 14 **"In the beginning was the Word, and the Word was with God, and the Word was God. (KJV)**

**The same was in the beginning with God.** verse 14 **"And the Word was made flesh, and dwelt among us, (and we beheld his glory, the glory as of the only begotten of the Father,) full of grace and truth.** (KJV) These verses should give us confidence in who we are because Jesus is who He is and He honors His word.

By the word became flesh means Jesus was completely God and completely man. By me reading the word like I do, I am putting on Christ.

**I John 1:1 "That which was from the beginning, which we have heard, which we have seen with our eyes, which we have looked upon, and our hands have handled, of the Word of life;** (KJV) This is the reason I belong to the Gideons International. They hand out the word of God to corporate America. Hospitals, Doctor's offices, Hotels and motels, to colleges and schools. Just think God is before us in creation, Jesus made the path clear with salvation, the blessed Holy Spirit lives within us in Sanctification and the word of God which we hold, it is for God and His instructions for us.

The Thursday night I got saved was a great experience. I went to the pool hall the next night with a buddy since we had an agreement to meet there on Friday nights. When I came home my dear wife of mine was at the door pointing her finger in my face saying, "You're not a Christian, because Christians don't play pool." Now where she got that I don't know. So I just politely got down on my knees and asked the Lord to come into my heart again. Nothing happened. The next night I did the same thing—nothing happened. I said, "Lord, You have to show me how I will know that I'm saved!" Over the next six months or so He did show me. Again God personalized the bible for me by giving me the following verses.

In 1 Corinthians 1:18 Paul wrote, **The preaching of the cross is to them that perish foolishness** [makes no sense]**; but unto us which are saved it is the power of God.**(KJV) I was acquainted with this, because I tried reading the Bible a few years before I was saved and it made no sense to me. Paul explained in 1 Corinthians 2:14, **The natural man** [the unsaved person] **receive not the things of the Spirit of God:** [the Spirit of God is not present in the unbeliever] **for they are foolishness** [make no sense] **unto him: neither can he know them, because they are spiritually discerned.**(KJV) This leads me to Romans 10:9–10: **If** [conditional on your part] **thou shalt confess with thy mouth the Lord Jesus,**

**and shalt believe in thine heart that God hath raised him** [Jesus] **from the dead, thou shalt be saved** (KJV) [it is a heart change, not a head change].

Once we receive Christ, He helps us with temptation. In 1 Corinthians 10:13 we read, **There hath no temptation taken you but such as is common to man** [You think you are the only one who has gone though what you are dealing with? Think again.]**: but God is faithful, who will not suffer you to be tempted above that ye are able; but will with the temptation** [not over it, under it, around it, but through it] **also make a way to escape, that ye may be able to bear it."** (KJV) The knowledge you gain from that temptation will carry you through many more temptations in this life.

The Lord fills us with His love, which naturally flows to others. In John 13:35 Jesus said, **By this shall all people know that ye are my disciples** [followers]**, if ye have love one to another** [overlooking their wrongdoings and shortcomings]. First John 3:14 reminds us, **We know that we have passed from death unto life, because we love the brethren. He that love not his brother abide in death."** (KJV) John 13:35 tells us that *people* will know, but 1 John 3;14 tells us that *we* will know. That was good enough for me in my personal salvation experience. Now all I needed was more information on the Bible being my everyday guide and God has done just that, In every way.

We have to know who we are before we can help others. This can be a very simple principle but very hard to detect. Satan does a great job hiding the simple truths of the Bible, especially to unbelievers and to the very weak in Christ. We need to examine ourselves to see where we are at, and where we come from and where we want to go. God will lead the way, if we will let Him.

Napoleon Hill tell us something that is worth repeating and worth chewing on like a cow with her cud:

**If you don't know why you failed, you are no wiser than when you began.**

There's an old adage that those who refuse to learn from history are doomed to repeat it. So it is with our failures. Unless we learn from our mistakes, we are likely to repeat them until we learn from such experiences and correct our course — or give up and accept temporary defeat as permanent failure. Every setback you encounter in life contains valuable information that, if you study it carefully, will eventually lead you to success. Without adversity, you would never develop wisdom, and without wisdom, success would be short-lived indeed. When you make a mistake, say, "That's good! I've gotten that out of the way. I will never do that again." You will no doubt make other mistakes, but they won't bother you nearly as much when you treat them as learning experiences.

Jesus tells us in Matthew 22:39, **Thou shalt love thy neighbor as thyself."** (KJV) In Ephesians 5 Paul tells husbands, **So ought men to love their wives as their own bodies. He that love his wife love himself."** (KJV) Now this love is a sacrifical love, a giving love, a love that God gives us—we are His creation.

Now let us touch base what the bible says about **love**. We have in the bible, a book of love in the Song of Solomon and a chapter of love in I Corinthians 13. Let us look at fifteen things God tells us about love in chapter 13: 4-8a 1. Love is patience, 2. love is kind, 3. love is not jealous, 4.

Love does not brag, 5. love is not arrogant, 6. love does not act unbecomingly, 7. Love does not seek her own, 8. Love is not provoked, 9. Love does not take into account a wrong suffered, 10. Love does not rejoice in unrighteousness, 11. Love rejoices with the truth: 12. Love bears all things, 12. Love believes things, (love can see in a heart, what is false and what is truth) 13. Love hope in all things, 14 love endures all things, 15. Love never fails: (NASV)

You can take these fifteen characteristics and I could type a while on just what love is. Lets looks at the same verses of I Corinthians 13: 4-8a: in other versions:

King James Version **4 Charity** (love) **suffereth long, and is kind; charity envieth not; charity vaunteth not itself, is not puffed up, 5 Doth not behave itself unseemly, seeketh not her own, is not easily provoked, thinketh no evil; 6 Rejoiceth not in iniquity, but rejoiceth in the truth; 7 Beareth all things, believeth all things, hopeth all things, endureth all things. 8 Charity never faileth** (KJV)

Christian Standard Bible 4 Love is patient, love is kind. Love does not envy, is not boastful, is not arrogant, **5** is not rude, is not self-seeking, is not irritable, and does not keep a record of wrongs. **6** Love finds no joy in unrighteousness but rejoices in the truth. **7** It bears all things, believes all things, hopes all things, endures all things **8** Love never ends." (CSB)

Easy-to-Read Version **4 Love is patient and kind. Love is not jealous, it does not brag, and it is not proud. 5 Love is not rude, it is not selfish, and it cannot be made angry easily. Love does not remember wrongs done against it. 6 Love is never happy when others do wrong, but it is** always happy with the truth. 7 Love never gives up on people. It never stops trusting, never loses hope, and never quits.8 Love will never end. (ERV)

English Standard Version 4 **Love is patient and kind; love does not envy or boast; it is not arrogant 5 or rude. It does not insist on its own way; it is not irritable or resentful;[a] 6 it does not rejoice at wrongdoing, but rejoices with the truth. 7 Love bears all things, believes all things, hopes all things, endures all things.8 Love never ends.** (ESV)

The Message **3-7 If I give everything I own to the poor and even go to the stake to be burned as a martyr, but I don't love, I've gotten nowhere. So, no matter what I say, what I believe, and what I do, I'm bankrupt without love, Love never gives up. Love cares more for others than for self. Love doesn't want what it doesn't have Love doesn't strut, Doesn't have a swelled head, Doesn't force itself on others, Isn't always "me first," Doesn't fly off the handle, Doesn't keep score of the sins of others, Doesn't revel when others grovel, Takes pleasure in the flowering of truth, Puts up with anything, Trusts God always, Always looks for the best, Never looks back, But keeps going to the end. 8-10 Love never dies. Inspired speech will be over some day; praying in tongues will end; understanding will reach its limit. We know only a portion of the truth, and what we say about God is always incomplete. But when the Complete arrives, our incompleteness will be canceled.** (MSG)

Revised Standard Version 4 **Love is patient and kind; love is not jealous or boastful; 5 it is not arrogant or rude.**

**Love does not insist on its own way; it is not irritable or resentful; 6 it does not rejoice at wrong, but rejoices in the right. 7 Love bears all things, believes all things, hopes all things, endures all things. 8 Love never ends.** (RSV)

The First Section

Now on to my birthday verses. These verses have carried me in God's family for the last five years now, and I share them in this little book, which is a great way to witness your friends. Like I said earlier in this book, With the meaning of my name being such, I just had to pick John 3:30 as my life's verse: **"He must increase, but I must decrease."** (KJV) Go figure that verse in front of you with the meaning of my name. With thirty-thousand-plus verses I had to pick that one. God has such humor. My life song is "At Calvary"— "Years I spent in vanity and pride, / Caring not my Lord was crucified, / Knowing not it was for me He died on Calvary. I can keep on my mind where I come from and who I was before I was saved.

Numbers in the Bible are most interesting to me. First, I love numbers. Second, there are divine spiritual lessons in the numbers of the Bible. For example, John 3:16, the most memorized verse in the Bible, has twenty-five words— twelve, twelve, and one. Let me give it to you this way: **For God so loved the world, that he gave his only begotten**— the first twelve words all deal with the holy God of the universe. This represents the Old Testament. The number 12 is an authoritative number. As long as the Jewish people obeyed the Lord, they had authority over the other countries around them. Let us skip over *Son* right now and go to the next twelve words, which represent Christ and all He did on the cross of Calvary: **that whosoever** [anyone who will call upon the name of Jesus] **believe in him should not perish** [to the unsaved will be their eternal home]**, but have everlasting life"** (KJV) [heaven as their eternal home]. These last twelve words represent the New Testament and what the Lord Jesus Christ did for you and me on the cross of Calvary. The one word that completes the twenty-five words of John 3:16 is the word "**Son**". The first twelve words look ahead and the last twelve look back to the Son and what He did on the cross of Calvary.

Now look at The Lord's Prayer. There are sixty-six words in that prayer in the King James Version, and there are sixty-six books in the Bible. How cool is that? God had it all planned out from the beginning of the ages.

Evangelist Ed F. Ballowe said in his book *Biblical Mathematics* that numbers are the secret code of God's Word. And also God's designing hand can be seen in the numbers. Yes, Dr. Ballowe and I both say learn to "count your Bible." Associations help you remember numbers. Being a number guy, I'll use a phone number. For example, let's use 867-244-4355. Look at the alphabetical letters under the numbers 2–9 on the number pad of your phone. For 1 use the asterisk and for 0 use the pound sign. Let's give it a try: you have three choices of letters to use for the number 8. We'll start with a consonant—there are twenty-one consonants in the English alphabet and five vowels. You can make good words like *top*–867, *big*–244 and *fell*–4355. There you have it for the ten numbers (867-244-4355)—top big fell. Sometimes it will not flow, but that's okay. For 1957 you could use a 1957 Chevrolet. Your brain can remember crazy things. Have fun playing with the phone numbers and the English alphabet.

Some of my birthday verses show my personality and some show who I really am deep down inside. I like the song "He's Still Working on Me."

We all have birthdays; therefore, you have a number of birthday verses. I hope you'll have as much fun with them as I did. I added the 3:16s into my birthday verses. First of all, they just fit. They seem to go with the flow as both in the pairs have a 16 in them.

Gateway Bible has 62 versions of the Holy bible on their site, I use them all in my birthday verses, kind of like the analogy of court. The lawyers get many witnesses' to tell their side of the story as they have seen it, so they can come up with a more accurate truth on the man/women they are trialing. Our English language has changed, the Greek and Hebrew have not. Like ye for our word you, or fetch for get, now we do use fetch when talking to our dog. I feel like our walk is strange enough for the unbelievers to handle, they do not need any strange talk too. Satan will use anything to discourage weak christians and sinners, we need to, by the Spirit's leading, keep ahead of our enemy. If different versions will do the trick, we are to use that version, but be very careful not to water down the word of God, which is also Satan's many tricks. People need to hear the pure truth of God's word.


Genesis 3:16; 9:16 Exodus 3:16; 9:16 Leviticus 3:16; 9:16

Numbers 9:16 Deuteronomy 3:16; 9:16 Joshua 3:16; 9:16 Judges 3:16; 9:16 Ruth 3:16 1 Samuel 3:16; 9:16 2 Samuel 3:16 1 Kings 3:16; 9:16 2 Kings 3:16; 9:16 1 Chronicles 3:16; 9:16 2 Chronicles 3:16; 9:16 Nehemiah 3:16; 9:16 Esther 9:16 Job 3:16; 9:16 Psalm 9:16 Proverbs 3:16; 9:16, Ecclesiastes 3:16; 9:16 Isaiah 3:16; 9:16 Jeremiah 3:16; 9:16 Lamentations 3:16 Ezekiel 3:16 Daniel 3:16; 9:16 Joel 3:16 Hosea 3:16 Nahum 3:16 Zephaniah 3:16, Habakkuk 3:16 Zechariah 9:16 Malachi 3:16 NT Matthew 3:16.9:16,

Mark 3:16, 9:19 Luke 3:16, 9:16, John 3:16, 9:16 Acts 3:16. 9:16 Romans 3:16, 9:16 I Corinthians 3:16, 9:16 II Corinthians 3;16, Galatians 3:16 Ephesians 3:16 Philippians 3:16 Colossians 3:16 2 Thessalonians 3:16 1Timothy 3:16 2 Timothy 3:16 Hebrews 3:16; 9:16 James 3:16 1 Peter 3:16

II Peter 3:16 1 John 3:16 Revelation 3:16:&; 9:16

Beginning from here I will use "OT" for the Old Testament and "NT" for the New. Verses quoted will be from the King James Version unless otherwise designated. There are twenty-eight books in the OT and twenty in the NT with a 3:16 reference.

The OT contains twenty-two books with a 9:16 reference and nine in the NT—for a total of thirty-one books.

First Section

**Day 1:** My first birthday verse in the Bible is Genesis 9:16: **The bow shall be in the cloud; and I will look upon it, that I may remember the everlasting covenant between God and every living creature of all flesh that is upon the earth.**(KJV) These thirty-four words have "remembering/the" as the center two words (everlasting covenant) Bible contains seven covenants, which fall into three categories: *conditional, unconditional* and *general.* The *conditional* covenants are based on certain obligations and prerequisites. If the requirements are not fulfilled, the covenant is broken. Five primary covenants are covenant (Genesis 6:18; 9:8–17): the Abrahamic covenant (Genesis

17:1–27); the Mosaic covenant (Exodus 19–24); and the David covenant (2 Samuel 7:5–16; Psalm 89, 132). Each of these covenants is reflective of two of the main categories of covenants known in the ancient Near East: the dealings with man and his God, and an agreement with God and man, conditional and unconditional.

In the NT you have two covenants: the new covenant or the new testament (the fulfillment of the promise God made to Israel to bring them back to the land and to help them obey the law (Luke 1:68–75—Zachariah speaking to his people, the Jews) and to restore fellowship with those whose hearts are turned toward Him. Covenant of Grace (Genesis 3:15; Isaiah 42:6)

I Genesis 3:15 God tells Adam, **I will put enmity between you and the woman, and between your seed and her** seed; **he shall bruise your head, and you shall bruise his heel** (KJV) [the nails prints in His hands and the hole in His side]. In Isaiah 42:6 God says, **I am the Lord; I have called you in righteousness; I will take you by the hand and keep you; I will give you as a covenant for the people, a light for the nations"** The new covenant is also   known as the better covenant, as referred to in Hebrews 8:6–7: **But now hath he** [Jesus] **obtained a more excellent ministry, by  how much also he is the mediator of a better covenant, which was established upon better promises. For if that first covenant had been faultless. then should no place have been sought for the second.** (KJV) In short, because Jesus went into heaven, He sent the comforter (the blessed Holy Spirit) to be a mediator. In 1 Timothy 2:5 we read, **There is one God, and one mediator between God and men, the man Christ Jesus.**

(KJV) This mediator or advocate is mentioned in 1 John 2:1–2: **My little children** [the Christians of John's time and we who are saved today]**, these things write I unto you, that ye sin not. And if any man sin, we have an advocate** [mediator] **with the Father, Jesus Christ the righteous: And he is the propitiation**(go between) **for our sins: and not for ours only, but also for the sins of the whole world.** (KJV)

This mediator or advocate is mentioned in 1 John 2:1–2: **My little children** [the Christians of John's time and we who are saved today]**, these things write I unto you, that ye sin not. And if any man sin, we have an advocate** [mediator] **with the Father, Jesus Christ the righteous: And he is the propitiation**(go between) **for our sins: and not for ours only, but also for the sins of the whole world.** (KJV)

In the NT we see Paul moving forward because he remembered where he was from and where he would be headed if it were not for Christ. Look at Paul's salvation experience described in Acts 22:3–8: **I am a Jew, born in Tarsus in Cilia, but brought up in this city, educated at the feet of Ngaliema according to the strict manner of the law of our fathers, being zealous for God as all of you are this day.** 4 **I persecuted this Way to the death, binding and delivering to prison both men and women,** 5 **as the high priest and the whole council of elders can bear me witness. From them I received letters to the brothers, and I journeyed toward Damascus to take those also who were there and bring them in bonds to Jerusalem to be punished.** 6 **As I was on my way and** drew near to Damascus, about noon a great light from heaven suddenly shone around me. 7 And I fell to the ground and heard a voice saying to me, "Saul, Saul, why are you persecuting me?" 8 And I answered, "Who are you, Lord?" And he said to me, "I am Jesus of Nazareth, whom you are persecuting" (ESV).

Peter recalled the mountaintop experience in these verses: 15 Moreover I will endeavor that ye may be able after my decease to have these things always in remembrance.16 For we have not followed cunningly devised fables, when we made known unto you the power and coming of our Lord Jesus Christ, but were eyewitnesses of his majesty. 17 For he received from God the Father honor and glory, when there came such a voice to him from the excellent glory, This is my beloved Son, in whom I am well pleased. 18 And this voice which came from heaven we heard, when we were with him in the holy mount 1I Peter 1:15–18 (KJV). This mountaintop experience, on what is called the Mount of Transfiguration, took place with Jesus as described in Mark 9:2–9 and Matthew 17:1–9. Such a revelation like that will sustain you a lifetime. It certainly made an impact on the three who had heard the voice from heaven.

In Luke 16:25 we read a story told by Jesus: But Abraham said, Son, remember that thou in thy lifetime received at thy good things, and likewise Lazarus evil things: but now he is comforted, and thou art tormented. (KJV) This alone will make that place hell. Prison is a mild form of hell because of men and women sitting in their jail cells simply *remembering*. The ark of remembering can be very good or it can be very bad.

Napoleon Hill wrote, "Only those who have the habit of going the second mile ever find the end of the rainbow."

It is a fact of life that most of us try and fail many times before we ultimately achieve the level of success we desire. You can expect to travel the extra mile many times only to find fool's gold at the end of your rainbow. But you will most certainly miss out on the great riches that await you if you quit trying. A superficial commitment to doing more than expected based only on what you expect to receive will not sustain you in the long term. Great achievement results from a commitment to do the right thing regardless of the consequences, and that commitment will ultimately lead you to the pot of gold at the end of your rainbow.

One more word before I leave the rainbow analogy. Don't try to explain it away with scientific facts. The more you say that, the more ingrained the rainbow becomes in my mind. All you're doing is proving that God can handle the elements of this old world for His purpose. After all, He made it in the first place.

**Theme:** Genesis is a book of beginnings that introduces central themes of the Bible, such as creation and redemption. (gateway bible)

**Overview:** The book of Genesis begins it all. It tells how God brought everything into being when there was no being to begin with. It starts with God, and that's the best place to start. From galactic wonder to terrestrial magnificence, God is the author of it all and He declares it all good. Then Genesis quickly describes how humans usher sin into creation and spoil it all. Yet, over and over in 50 chapters we see how God worked to redeem humanity through the imperfect and dysfunctional families of the biblical patriarchs of Noah, Abraham, Isaac, Jacob, and Joseph. Filled with thrilling stories and grand messages, as the <u>NIV Study Bible</u> says, Genesis is supremely a book that speaks about relationships: between God and his creation, between God and humankind, and between human beings. (gateway bible)

Other versions of Genesis 9:16

Easy-to-Read Version: **"When I look and see the rainbow in the clouds, I will remember the agreement that continues forever. I will remember the agreement between me and every living thing on the earth."** (ERV)

The Living Bible: **16-17 "For I will see the rainbow in the cloud and remember my eternal promise to every living being on the earth."** (TLB)

The Message: vs.12-16 **"God continued, "This is the sign of the covenant I am making between me and you and everything living around you and everyone living after you. I'm putting my rainbow in the clouds, a sign of the covenant between me and the Earth. From now on, when I form a cloud over the Earth and the rainbow appears in the cloud, I'll remember my covenant between me and you and everything living, that never again will floodwaters destroy all life. When the rainbow appears in the cloud, I'll see it and remember the eternal covenant between God and everything living, every last living creature."** (MSG)

World English Bible: **"The rainbow will be in the cloud. I will look at it, that I may remember the everlasting covenant between God and every living creature of all flesh that is on the earth."** (WEB)

Wycliffe Bible: "And my bow shall be in the clouds, and I shall see it, and I shall have mind of the everlasting bond of peace, which is made between God and man, and each soul living of all flesh which is on earth. (And my rainbow shall be in the clouds, and I shall see it, and I shall remember the everlasting covenant, which is made between God and man, and each living soul of all the kinds of flesh that be on the earth.)" (WYC)

Genesis 3:16 "Unto the woman he said, I will greatly multiply thy sorrow and thy conception; in sorrow thou shalt bring forth children; and thy desire shall be to thy husband, and he shall rule over thee. (KJV) We have in 3:16 a woman giving birth to a newborn and in 9:16 we have protection for all mankind, from a worldwide flood.

**Day 2:** My next birthday verse is Exodus 9:16: **And in very deed for this cause have I raised thee** (Moses) **up, for to shew in thee my power; and that my name may be declared throughout all the earth.** (KJV) It's in the book of Exodus we read about the Jews' escape out of Egypt, their hell on earth. Exodus 9:16 has thirty words in the KJV version. Some versions use more, some less. I am not against any other versions, but some destroy the true meaning by using words like *young maiden* instead of *virgin*. There is no comparison—a young maiden can be a virgin or she can be a young harlot of the street. We are responsible for God's Word and the full meaning of this Word He has for us. Satan knows the word and wants to destroy its full meaning of His power and of His glory.

In Isaiah 9:16 we see God's power and His name. I want

to give you two or three verses for each. First we will look at God's power. **His** [Jesus's] **invisible attributes, namely, his eternal power and divine nature, have been clearly perceived, ever since the creation of the world, in the things that have been made. So they** [sinners] **are without excuse** (Romans 1:20 ESV). **I** [Paul] **am not ashamed of the gospel, for it is the power of God for salvation to everyone who believes, to the Jew first and also to the Greek** Romans 1:16 ESV. Saints are saved, kept, and constantly empowered for life and ministry. **May the God of hope fill you** [the Christian] **with all joy and peace in believing, so that by the power of the Holy Spirit you may abound in hope. . . .** 19 **By the power of signs and wonders, by the power of the Spirit of God, so that from Jerusalem and all the way around to Curriculum I have fulfilled the ministry of the gospel of Christ** (Romans 15:13, 19 ESV). I could go on and on, but you're getting the picture. Now—God's name is proclaimed in all the earth. **Heaven and earth will pass away, but my words** [name] **will not pass away** (Matthew 24:35 ESV). In John 1:1 we read of Jesus, **In the beginning was the Word, and the Word was with God, and was God.**(KJV) We cannot separate God and His Word. When you see one you should see the other. Jesus said in John 14:13, **Whatever you ask in my name, this I will do, that the Father may be glorified in the Son.** (KJV)

We pray in Jesus's name: **On that day you will ask nothing of me. Truly, truly, I say to you, whatever you ask of the Father in my name, he will give it to you** (John 16:23 ESV). **I will make all my goodness pass before**

**thee, and I will proclaim the name of the Lord before thee** (Exodus 33:19 (KJV).

**Theme:** God reveals himself to His people and delivers them from slavery in Egypt to establish a covenant with them in the desert. (gateway bible)

**Overview:** A spectacular escape and a hair-raising chase scene are only two of the many riveting stories in the book of Exodus. The **NIV Quest Study Bible** says this book is more than

an epic adventure with Moses as its central character; it also recounts God's supernatural rescue of the Israelites from oppression in Egypt. Despite God's miraculous intervention, the

Israelites did not remain loyal to Him and ended up wandering in the desert for 40 years. The book recounts how God revealed His name, His attributes, and His redemption. It's where we find the Passover story and Ten Commandments. Israel's faltering faith reminds us that even imperfect people can get to know the God who loves them perfectly. The story of Exodus establishes themes of rescue and redemption that are repeated in both the Old and New Testaments. (gateway bible)

We have a purpose for being here. In his book *The Purpose Driven Life* Rick Warren tells us to find our SHAPE: S—spiritual gifts (the Bible mentions several); H—heart; A—abilities; P—personality; and E—experience. If you are willing, God can do all this and more for you.

The theme of Warren's book focuses on God's purposes for your life. He lists five:

Purpose one: You were planned for God's pleasure.

Purpose two: You were formed for God's family.

Purpose three: You were created to become like Christ.

Purpose four: You are shaped for serving God.

Purpose five: You were made for a mission.

You are somebody! God wants you in His service, serving Him for life. Satan will try to drag you down and get you to believe the lie that you are a nobody. That is why I read huge amounts of scripture each day, to be reminded of my place in God's family. I might not feel like it, but I cannot and will not trust my feelings.

Exodus 3:16 **"Go, and gather the elders of Israel together, and say unto them, The Lord God of your fathers, the God of Abraham, of Isaac, and of Jacob, appeared unto me, saying, I have surely visited you, and seen that which is done to you in Egypt:** (KJV)

Moses was God's man, to lead the Israelites to the promise land. we see this in both 3:16 and 9:16

Other versions of the bible on Exodus 9:16:

The Message: ". **But for one reason only I've kept you on your feet: To make you recognize my power so that my reputation spreads in all the Earth.**" (MSG)

The Living Bible:" **But I didn't, for I wanted to demonstrate my power to you and to all the earth.**" (TLB)

English Standard Version: **"But for this purpose I have raised you up, to show you my power, so that my name may be proclaimed in all the earth."** (ESV)

Wycliffe Bible: **"forsooth therefore I have set thee, that I show my strength in thee, and that my name be told** (out) **in each land. (yea, I have kept thee alive, only so that I could show my strength through thee, and**

**so that my name would be spoken of in every land.)"** (WYC)

**Day 3:** In Leviticus 9:16 we read, **And he** [the priest] **brought the burnt offering, and offered it according to the manner.**(KJV) There is a form and manner of doing things in God's kingdom. Leviticus 9:16 contains thirteen words. The middle word is *and.* What do you do with that word? God is God <u>and</u> He wants me to be part of His work and His family. Each word is valuable. You have 783,137 words in the KJV, 782,815 in the NASB, 770,430 in the NIV, 727,969 in the ESV. You have the trimming-down of words in each of the versions that I mention. Now I am not saying to throw out all versions except for the KJV—just be careful in keeping the true message that God has for you. You have 54,846 word differences in these versions, which can be huge in the meaning of each version claiming to carry the true Word of God.

**Theme:** The Israelistes receive instructions from God at the base of Mount Sinai concerning how to live as God's holy people. (gateway bible)

**Overview:** Any functional society needs laws to govern its population to avoid disintegrating into anarchy. The **NIV Quest Study Bible** says at first glance, the book of Leviticus may seem like an out-of-date legal document describing unsavory customs. But a larger view reveals how the book allowed Israel to maintain a right relationship with God and preserve its distinctiveness from the wayward nations around it. These laws provided a guide for "set apart" living and a means of dealing with sin and its destructive consequences. Scholars have debated for centuries which of these laws still apply to Christians, but don't get bogged down in the "legalese" of Leviticus. Instead, read it for the big picture—to get a better understanding of God's holiness and his gift of salvation as portrayed in Israel's sacrificial system. (Gateway bible)

Now back to Leviticus 9:16. The priest had work to do in the service of God and He carried it on according to the dues at hand. We each have duties to perform, and we will be wise to carry them out according to the Word of God just as in a family unit, where each has his or her duties to carry out. We read of the clothes that the priest wore to the duties he performed. The message of God was told by the clothes he wore to the services that he carried out, and the message was clear. We read that the priest was thirty years old when he started serving, and he served until he reached the age of fifty. We read that it was the priests who were responsible for Jesus's death: **And as soon as it was day, the elders of the people and the chief priests and the scribes came together, and led him into their council saying, Art thou the Christ?** (Luke 22:66–67 KJV). What? They should have known this already. The scribes were the ones who copied the words of the Scriptures. Did they not learn from them that Christ was to come and die for the sins of the whole world? They, as all others, got lax in their duties and calling. We also, if not careful, will let our guard down and forget who we represent. In the OT the priests came from the tribe of the Levites. In the NT the priests are all the believers in Christ. The words of 2 Peter 2:9 tell me that I am a priest: **You are a chosen generation, a royal priesthood, an holy nation, a peculiar people; that you should shew forth the praises of him who hath called you out of darkness**

**into his marvelous light.**(KJV) What a verse! And that, my friend, is one of many thousands found in the Scriptures. Let us break it down into little bites. First—you are chosen. **According as he** [Jesus] **hath chosen us in him before the foundation of the world, that we should be holy and without blame before him in love** (Ephesians 1:4 KJV). As stated in the second greatest commandment, we are to love one another as ourselves. Jesus tells His disciples in John 15:16, **Ye have not chosen me, but I have chosen you, and ordained you, that ye should go and bring forth fruit, and that your fruit should remain: that whatsoever ye shall ask of the Father in my name, he may give it you.** (KJV)

Fifty or so years ago Jesus came to me and saved me. I was the first in my immediate family to be saved. Since then I was a part in my older sister's salvation; she was killed in a car accident two months later. Then my father and mother were saved. Daddy was fifty-nine years old and mom was fifty-five. I hope I was a shining light to my two older twin brothers, both of whom are now deceased along with mom and dad.

Next, in 1 Peter 2:9 we read, **Ye are . . . a royal priesthood** [those who do priestly work, being busy in church and for God's kingdom]. Being a priest was a calling, just as salvation is a calling. Being a priest was one thing, but being a *royal priesthood* carries a lot more responsibility. Let us guard this position God has given us. **An holy nation**—I like to think of America as being a holy nation, and I will do my part in keeping it so.

Let me get political for a minute. We as Americans have the opportunity to vote for our leaders, so we need to exercise that right. America was founded on religious freedom. We are allowed to worship God freely. As Christians we are **a peculiar people** to the world, and to the unsaved. The world just doesn't understand us, our talk, or our walk. All we do is so far removed from their lifestyles. Jesus while on this earth was a rejected, considered an illegitimate child, the simple son of a carpenter, perhaps a mama's boy. All these presumptions came from the religious crowd. At every turn the Pharisees were trying to trip Him up, confuse the words He spoke and to get Him on what He was doing, like picking corn or healing people on the Sabbath day. Yes! We are a peculiar people—or if not, we *should* be, to the world's crowds, that is.

We ought to be so busy doing His will and praising Him **without blame** (shame) (Ephesians 1:4 KJV). How can I do that? **When a man's ways please the Lord, he market even his enemies to be at peace with him** (Proverbs 16:7). Jesus said in Matthew 5:48, **Be ye therefore perfect, even as your father which is in heaven is perfect.**(KJV) These two verses are impossible to keep within yourself. We need the Lord to step in, walk with us, and guide us.

Leviticus 3:16 **"And the priest shall burn them upon the altar: it is the food of the offering made by fire for a sweet savour: all the fat is the Lord's.** Both in 3:16 and 9:16 we see the work of the Priest.

Other versions of the bible of Leviticus 9:16:

The Message: **"He presented the Whole-Burnt-Offering following the same procedures." (MSG)**

Names of God Bible: **"Following the proper procedures, he brought forward the burnt offering and sacrificed it."** (NGB)

International Standard Version: **"Then he brought the whole burnt offering and offered it according to procedure"** (ISV)

Jubilee Bible 2000: **"And he brought the burnt offering and offered it according to the ordinance."** (JUB)

**Day 4: Numbers 9:16 reads, So it was away: the cloud covered it by day, and the appearance of fire by night.** (KJV) Seventeen words make up this verse, the middle being *day*. **God created the day and night on the first day of creation (Genesis 1:5).** Everyone can look out the window on a clear night and see the moon and stars shining down, sometimes almost giving the appearance of day. The light of the moon and stars shows us that God has not left us in complete darkness. Sinners are of the night and cannot see, while the saved ones are of the *day* and *can* see. Paul tells us that while we Christians are on this earth, we see through a glass darkly the things pertaining to heaven 1 Corinthians 13:12. **For he knoweth our frame; He remembereth that we are dust** (Psalm 103:14 KJV). Next time we get the big head, let's just remember: we are just dust—holy dust—that is, that's going to heaven. In Genesis it tells us that dust you are and dust will you return. Just think of that when we get the big head, **we are only dirt.**

**Theme:** Because the Israelites are unwilling to enter the land of Canaan, their entire generation is forced to wander in the Desert of Sinai for 38 years. (gateway bible)

**Overview:** Reading a book titled "Numbers" may sound about as exciting as reading a dictionary or paging through a phone book, but get ready for a surprise: this book is loaded with powerful stories. The **NIV Quest Study Bible** says it graphically illustrates what happens when people sin, but it also exemplifies hope for those who desire God's mercy and want to experience his faithfulness. The book of Numbers reveals a God of devastating wrath who also holds his arms wide open for those who repent of their sin and turn to him. Within this book you'll find the Israelites' repeated cycles of sin, judgment, and repentance. You'll see not only human failure but also God's patient and merciful response. This book shows the lengths to which God goes to love and rescue his people. (gateway bible)

Numbers 3:16 **"And Moses numbered them according to the word of the Lord, as he was commanded.** (KJV) We see God's protection to His people the Jews, the cloud and fire and they were numbered. We all as a number have something to do with God"s ever looking eye on us.

Other versions on Numbers 9:16

American Standard Version: **So it was alway: the cloud covered it, and the appearance of fire by night."** (ASV)

Amplified Bible: **"So it was continuously; the cloud covered it *by day*, and the appearance of fire by night."** (AMP)

Amplified Bible, Classic Edition: **"So it was constantly; the cloud covered it by day, and the appearance of fire by night. ."** (AMC)

BRG Bible: **"So it was alway: the cloud covered it *by day*, and the appearance of fire by night."** (BRG)

**Day 5: In Deuteronomy 9:16 we read, And I l(Moses) looked, and behold, ye had sinned against the Lord your God, and had made you a molten calf: ye had turned aside quickly out of the way which the Lord had commanded you."** (KJV) This thirty-five-word verse shows how we as humans can and will be if left to ourselves. It tells us that the Hebrews turned aside quickly. God has given us a clear command to follow. As Rick Warren points out, Like the song says "we were born to serve the Lord". However, we are born in sin: **"Behold, I was shape in iniquity; and in sin did my mother conceive me."** (Psalm 51:5 KJV).

**Theme:** In a series of farewell messages, Moses exhorts the new generation of Israelites to live as his obedient people in the promised land. (gateway bible)

**Overview:** As you read the 34 chapters in the book of Deuteronomy, you'll see how God's people dealt not only with hardship, testing, and doubt but also with promise, hope, and trust. It tells us that faith is not automatic or mechanical. Faith becomes personal and active when it springs from a living relationship with a loving God. The **NIV Quest Study Bible** says the message of Deuteronomy can be summed up this way: devote yourself wholeheartedly to God. In the book, Moses commands his readers to "love the Lord your God with all your heart and with all your soul and with all your strength" (6:5). He challenged the people to faithfully obey the Lord and reject all forms of idolatry. He called on the new generation to formally renew the earlier covenant with God that their parents had broken. (gateway bible)

Deuteronomy 3:16 **"And unto the Reubenites and unto the Gadites I gave from Gilead even unto the river Arnon half the valley, and the border even unto the river Jabbok, which is the border of the children of Ammon;** (KJV) God give land to the 2-1/2 tribes of Judah and in chapter 9:16 they still sin against the Lord. Sounds all so familiar does it not. We forget too easily, the countless blessings that God gives us day by day.

Other versions of the bible dealing with Deuteronomy 9:16:

Christian Standard Bible: **"I saw how you had sinned against the Lord your God; you had made a calf image for yourselves. You had quickly turned from the way the Lord had commanded for you."** (CSB)

Common English Bible: **"It was then that I saw how you sinned against the Lord your God: you made yourselves a calf, an idol made of cast metal! You couldn't wait to turn from the path the Lord commanded you! ."** (CEB)

Complete Jewish Bible: **"I looked, and there, you had sinned against *Adonai* your God! You had made yourselves a metal calf, you had turned aside quickly from the way *Adonai* had ordered you to follow."** (CJB)

New Revised Standard Version Catholic Edition: **"Then I saw that you had indeed sinned against the Lord your God, by casting for yourselves an image of a calf; you had been quick to turn from the way that the Lord had commanded you. ."** (NRSVCE)

There you have the five books of Moses' Pentateuch, the Jewish law. Time of Moses's writing of the five books of the law is somewhere from 1446 to 1406 BC

**Day 6:** In Joshua 9:16 we read, **And it came to pass at the end of three days after they had made a league with them, that they heard that they were their neighbors, and that they dwelt among them.** (KJV)

This is what happens to us if we do not consult the Lord on transactions we engage in. We can get ourselves in a mess really fast. Joshua 9:3-6 tells us 3 **And when the inhabitants of Gibeon heard what Joshua had done unto Jericho and to Ai,** 4 **They did work wilily, and went and made as if they had been ambassadors, and took old sacks upon their asses, and wine bottles, old, and rent, and bound up;** 5 **And old shoes and clouted upon their feet, and old garments upon them; and all the bread of their provision was dry and mouldy.** 6 **And they went to Joshua unto the camp at Gilgal, and said unto him, and to the men of Israel, We be come from a far country: now therefore make ye a league with us.**(KJV)

Proverbs 22:3 tells us a wise person who knows the Word of God: **A prudent man forseeth evil, and hide himself: but the simple pass on, and are punished.**(KJV) Proverbs 27:12 repeats these words. Solomon did not want us to miss this simple truth. Christians should know both how to hide from evil and how to face evil. They were setting up Joshua and his men. The same thing happens today: people will lie, cheat, and misguide you in anything that is to their favor or advantage. The Good Book tells us to be wise as serpents and harmless as doves.

The Lord uses two types of living things that we know a lot about. Serpents are very wise in their goings—that is why Satan used the serpent in the garden to trip up Eve. Doves, on the other hand, are lowly, meek, and humble. They are graceful in their flight and peaceful in their ways. Also in another place the Bible tells us that a sluggard man or woman upon his or her bed can outwit you by seven fold if given a chance as the Gideonites did. They can dream up more ways to outsmart you, or they think they can.

Some people will work harder on that than simply getting a real job.

Proverbs 14:12 says, **There is a way which seemeth right unto a man, but the end thereof are the ways of death.** (KJV) In Proverbs 21:2 we read, **Every way of a man is right in his own eyes: but the Lord ponderer the hearts.** (KJV) Both of these verses have an action and a promise from God for the outcome. What is in your heart? Only the Lord and you know. The Bible tells us that the heart is wicked: **The heart is deceitful above all things, and desperately wicked: who can know it?** (Jeremiah 17:9 KJV). It's shocking that I don't understand my own heart. Have you ever said that to yourself? What's wrong with me? Why did I do that? Romans 7:14–24 will tell you. You will find this quoted and a full explanation near the beginning of this book. As the song says in "Sweet hour of Prayer " What peace we often forfeit because we do not take it to the Lord in prayer.

**Theme:** God enables Joshua to lead the armies of Israel to victory over the Canaanites in the promised land. (gateway bible)

**Overview:** "Have you ever wished for a second chance? Maybe you squandered a rare opportunity. Maybe you tried something, but your attempt failed. Or maybe you wasted a precious gift or a valued friendship. The <u>NIV Quest Study Bible</u> says the book of Joshua reminds us that God often offers us a second chance. Though the Israelites failed to enter the promised land the first time because of their lack of faith, and though they wasted 40 years because of their failure, God gave the next generation another opportunity. The Israelites had learned their lesson, and the results were different the second time around. In the book we also learn more about God, including his purposes and how he works in human lives. The book of Joshua is where we're told to **"Be strong and courageous. Do not be afraid; do not be discouraged, for the Lord your God will be with you wherever you go** (Joshua 1:9). (gateway bible)

Other versions that deals with Joshua 9:16

Contemporary English Version: verses 16-17 **"A couple of days later,[a] the Israelites found out that these people actually lived in the nearby towns of Gibeon, Chephirah, Beeroth, and Kiriath-Jearim.[b] So the Israelites left the place where they had camped and arrived at the four towns two days later.[c]"** (CEV)

Darby Translation: **"And it came to pass at the end of three days after they had made a covenant with them, that they heard that they were their neighbours, and that they dwelt in their midst."** (DARBY)\

Easy-to-Read Version: **"Three days later the Israelites learned that these men lived very near their camp."** (ERV)

Evangelical Heritage Version: **"But three days after they had made the treaty with them, the Israelites heard that they were their neighbors, that is, that they were living among them."** (EHV)

**Day 7:** Our next birthday verse is found in Judges 9:16 **Now therefore, if ye have done truly and sincerely, in that ye have made Abimelech king, and if ye have dealt well with Jerusalem and his house, and have done unto him according to the deserving of his hands.** (KJV) This verse makes more sense it we added verse 17 to it, which says, **"For my father fought for you, and adventured his**

**life far, and delivered you out of the hand of Midian".** (KJV) **T**he book of Judges deals with the Jews' desire for what the other nations have: an earthly king. The judges kept the people from themselves, from sinning against God. When God finally allowed them to have a king, then we see the people going back into their old ways of sin. Everybody needs somebody to keep him or her on the straight and narrow path, such as an accountability partner, or the Bible itself. God will not leave us forsaken or without a clear path to Him. Judges is the seventh book of the OT and in this book God deals with His people with and by the judges He set up.

Back to Judges 9:16: **Now therefore, if ye have done truly and sincerely, in that ye have made Abimelech king** (Abimelech was a righteous king, whose name means "father of the king"], **and if ye (You) have dealt well with Jerusalem** [this was Gideon, a military leader, judge, and prophet whose calling and victory over the Canaanites are recounted in Judges 5–8) **and his house, and have done unto him according to the deserving of his hands.**(KJV) This verse is unique in that in verse 14 you have the parable of the bramble speaking. How cool is that, being that I am a Bramble? Let me just quote verses 14–15 leading up to verse 16: **Then said all the trees unto the *bramble*, Come thou, and reign over us. And the *bramble* said unto the trees, If in truth ye anoint me king over you, then come and put your trust in my shadow: and if not, let fire come out of the *bramble,* and devour the cedars of Lebanon** (emphasis added). The bramble bush here seen an opening and was going to take advantage of it. Judges 9:16 has thirty nine words in it and the middle word is Ye (You) five times. Do you see the word ye or you in Judges 9:16. Five stands for grace, but the brambles were not gracious in their demands, they wanted complete authority. Now, the brambles had stipulations on how and why they were to follow. The Jews wanted a king like the neighbors around them and the bramble bush was getting on the voting ballot

Now this points out one of my faults, that of being bossy and like a dictator. I found myself as a Christian like Paul in Romans 7:24: **O wretched man that I am!** (KJV) In Judges 9:16 you have several stipulations to follow, the forerunner of what was ahead of Israel when they wanted a king. In 1 Samuel 8:1–19 God told the Jews through His prophet Samuel that He, the king, would have stipulations. But they would not hearken unto Samuel. Let us get back to the bramble and His stipulations. Number one: **Come and put your trust in my shadow.** Not good, putting your trust in one person other than the person of the Godhead. Number two: **If not, let fire come out of the *bramble,* and devour the cedars of Lebanon** (KJV) (emphasis added). A little too judgmental, don't you think? God was trying to forewarn the Jewish people of the dangers of having a king. It might look good and smell good, but the bad would outweigh the good.

Today I am a son of Joe Bramble and the significance of the Bramble name I will carry out—good, bad, or indifferent. It is the males who carry the last name, to populate and to be the class of people they want their last names to represent or to be remembered by. Jesse James did not set a good example for the James' clan. On the other hand, Abraham Lincoln set a good example for the Lincoln family. Whether James or Lincoln, the rest of the males in James' clan have to set

46

that name straight—good, bad, or indifferent. We all want a good name, but there is a price to pay, are we up to do it?

**Theme:** In danger of losing the promised land, the Israelite's are delivered again and again by God through leaders known as "judges. (gateway bible)

**Overview:** Covering a period of about 350 years in the centuries before Christ, the book of Judges is filled with stories as sensational and dramatic as any of today's headlines. The **NIV Quest Study Bible** says that, In terms of sheer spectacle—gruesome murders, sexual exploits, superhuman feats of strength, bizarre mutilation—no tabloid of today could offer you more. But no tabloid could offer the eternal truth you'll find within these stories. The book of Judges says, "When they cried out to the Lord, he raised up for them a deliverer" (3:9). It shows what happened when Israel repeatedly slid into moral anarchy, and it highlights God's merciful deliverance when his people cry out to him in repentance. (gateway bible)

Now let's compare other versions of Judges 9:16:

Douay-Rheims 1899 American Edition: **"Now therefore if you have done well, and without sin in appointing Abimelech king over you, and have dealt well with Jerobaal, and with his house, and have made a suitable return for the benefits of him, who fought for you,"** (DRA)

Easy-to-Read Version: **"Now if you were completely honest when you made Abimelech king, may you be happy with him. And if you have been fair to Gideon and his family, and if you have treated him as you should, this is also goo**d." (ERV)

Evangelical Heritage Version**: "Jotham said, "So**

now, if you acted in truth and integrity when you made Abimelek king, and if you have treated Jerubbaal and his household well, and if you have dealt with him." *EHV)

English Standard Version: **"Now therefore, if you acted in good faith and integrity when you made Abimelech king, and if you have dealt well with Jerubbaal and his house and have done to him as his deeds deserved—"** (ESV)

**Day 8:** In 1 Samuel 9:16 we read, **To morrow about this time I will send thee a man out of the land of Benjamin, and thou shalt anoint him to be captain over my people Israel, that he may save my people out of the hand of the Philistines: for I have looked upon my people, because their cry is come unto me.** (KJV) In this lengthy verse of fifty-seven words, the middle being the word *Israel* (God's chosen people), God was talking to Samuel to go and anoint their first leader, Saul. Notice that *Israel* has the three letters of our financial agency in it: "IRS," like Jerusalem, the city of God: Jer/usa/lem. No, my friend, this is no fluke, God knows what He is doing. God will use America if Americans will stay faithful to Jerusalem. You know the story of Saul and his rage and jealousy over David, who would eventually be the second king. But while he was alive he put Israel through the paces. Saul was a Benjamite and a military leader who was to fight the Canaanites. The Philistines were enemies of Israel. God heard their cry and He had compassion on them, knowing the outcome. God will give us what we really want if we insist, even if it is bad for us, to teach us valuable lessons. God is gracious and wants to bless us, but we need to be patient and wait on His timing.

The Jewish people wanted a king to keep up with their neighbors. This was the wrong goal.

**Theme:** The nation of Israel transitions from being led by God through "judges" to being led by him through kings. (gateway bible)

**Overview:** According to playwright Arthur Miller, a great play is one in which you discover your own characteristics in the drama's actors. The **NIV Quest Study Bible** says, in the books of first and second Samuel we find heroic stories and colorful characters. As we experience their tragedies and triumphs, their emotional highs and lows, we learn more about ourselves—and how God wants to work in our lives. In 1 Samuel we're introduced to, and follow the lives of, Eli the priest, Samuel the prophet, King Saul, his son Jonathan, young David, and Goliath the giant. Each of the book's main characters has flaws and strengths. Some are blessed by God while others receive his judgment. The book ends with the death of King Saul. (gateway bible)

I Samuel 3:16 **Then Eli called Samuel, and said, Samuel, my son. And he answered, "Here am I."** (KJV) In 3:16 we see the calling of Samuel and in 9:16 we see the calling of Saul. Samuel was a good prophet and Saul bad king. Samuel a gracious man and Saul a greedy man

Other versions deals with I Samuel 9:16:

1599 Geneva Bible **"Tomorrow about this time I will send thee a man out of the land of Benjamin, him shalt thou anoint to be governor over my people Israel, that he may save my people out of the hands of the Philistines; for I have looked upon my people, and their cry is come unto me.** (GNV)

GOD'S WORD Translation **"About this time**

tomorrow I will send you a man from the territory of Benjamin. Anoint him to be ruler of my people Israel. He will save my people from the Philistines because I've seen my people's suffering and their cry has come to me." (GW)

Good News Translation **"Tomorrow about this time I will send you a man from the tribe of Benjamin; anoint him as ruler of my people Israel, and he will rescue them from the Philistines. I have seen the suffering of my people and have heard their cries for help."** (GNT

Holman Christian Standard Bible **"At this time tomorrow I will send you a man from the land of Benjamin. Anoint him ruler over My people Israel. He will save them from the hand of the Philistines because I have seen the affliction of My people, for their cry has come to Me."** (HCSB)

**Day 9:** First Kings 9:16 **"For Pharaoh king of Egypt had gone up, and taken Geezer, and burnt it with fire, and slain the Canaanites that dwelt in the city, and given it for a present unto his daughter, Solomon's wife.** (KJV) Solomon had married into idolatry, women who served strange gods. God had warned against mixed marriages: **"Neither shalt thou make marriages with them; thy daughter thou shalt not give unto his son, nor his daughter shalt thou take unto thy son."** (Deuteronomy 7:3 KJV). Of the nations concerning which the Lord said unto the children of Israel, **"Ye shall not go in to them, neither shall they come in unto you: for surely they will turn away your heart after their gods: Solomon clung unto**

these in love" (1 Kings 11:2 KJV). Solomon apparently did not care what God had to say about heathen women. God gives boundaries on marriage both in the OT and the NT. He forbids Christians to marry non-Christians. If you are already married to a nonbeliever, God gives instructions on this, How she/he can be won by your conduct or by actions.

If at death a mate dies, **She is at liberty to be married to whom she will; only in the Lord** (1 Corinthians 7:39 KJV). In 1 Corinthians 7 Paul tells about the unbelievers and believers who are married and what to do in that case. God wants us to marry believers. He also gives courting instructions in the Song of Solomon. The sexual instruction in Hebrews 13:4 is as follows: **Marriage is honorable in all, and the bed undefined: but whore mongers and adulterers God will judge.** (KJV)

Let me say that God is gracious God and will allow us to make mistakes like with our marriages. Like me for instance, I have been married three times and God has forgiven me, I am in His submissive will, which is far better than not being saved at all. I can do as much as a person who has never been divorce His or he's testimony can be stronger than mine but we will be in heaven together. God looks at the heart.

Marriage is honorable and God recognizes it. Truly there will be a judgment day: **But I say unto you, That every idle word that men shall speak, they shall give account thereof in the day of judgment** (Matthew 12:36 KJV). What a sobering thought—that is, every idle word spoken in anger, words that do not lift up, these words will be judged! In Revelation 20:11–15 we read, 11 **And I saw a great white throne, and him that sat on it, from whose** face the earth and the heaven fled away; and there was found no place for them.12 And I saw the dead, small and great, stand before God; and the books were opened: and another book was opened, which is the book of life: and the dead were judged out of those things which were written in the books, according to their works.13 And the sea gave up the dead which were in it; and death and hell delivered up the dead which were in them: and they were judged every man according to their works. 14 And death and hell were cast into the lake of fire. This is the second death. And whosoever was not found written in the book of life was cast into the lake of fire. (KJV) God judges sin.

In Romans 14:10 we read, **But why dost thou judge thy brother? or why dost thou set at nought thy brother? for we shall all stand before the judgment seat of Christ.** (KJV) In John 12:48 Jesus says, **He that reject me, and receiveth not my words, hath one that judgeth him: the word that I have spoken, the same shall judge him on the last day.** (KJV) In Acts 17:31 we read, **Because *he* hath appointed a day, in the which *he* will judge the world in righteousness by that man whom *he* hath ordained; whereof *he* hath given assurance unto all men, in that *he* hath raised *him* from the dead** KJV(emphasis added). Six times the Lord is mentioned by the pronoun *He* or *Him*.

*This verse in I Kings 9:16 is special to me because it is the ninth birthday verse in the old testament, being September is the ninth month of the year.*

**Theme:** After Solomon's death, the nation is divided into the northern kingdom (Israel) and the southern kingdom (Judah). (gateway bible)

**Overview:** The story of King Solomon—famous for his great wisdom and infamous for his polygamy—is described in the book of First Kings, along with accounts of other sovereigns who ruled when the kingdom was divided into the ten northern tribes of Israel and the two southern tribes of Judah. The **NIV Quest Study Bible** says these kings provide us with both positive role models to follow and negative examples to avoid. The book begins with the last days of David, then describes the reign and fall of his son Solomon and the division of his kingdom upon his death. We also meet extraordinary characters like the prophets Elijah and Elisha, and are told of Elijah's confrontation with King Ahab and his taunting of the prophets of Baal. First and second Kings were originally one book. First Kings ends shortly after the deaths of Ahab of the northern kingdom and Jehoshaphat of the southern kingdom. According to the **NIV quest Study Bibl**e placing the division at this point causes the account of the reign of Ahaziah of Israel to overlap the end of 1 Kings and the beginning of 2 Kings. The same is true of the narration of the ministry of Elijah, which for the most part appears in 1 Kings. (gateway bible)

I Kings 3:16 "**Then came there two women, that were harlots, unto the king, and stood before him.**" (KJV) This verse is the starting of the wisdom of King Solomon with the two women and their babies, This story continues through verse 28. We see in this chapter God gives Solomon wisdom and in chapter 9 we see Solomon's father-in-law give a present to his heaven daughter, Solomon's wife.

Other bible versions that deals with I Kings 9:16:

*The International Children's Bible:* **In the past the king of Egypt had attacked Gezer and captured it. He had** burned it and killed the Canaanites who lived there. Then he gave it to his daughter as a wedding present. His daughter married Solomon." (ICB)

International Standard Version: "**Pharaoh, the king of Egypt, had attacked and captured Gezer, burned it down, killed the Canaanites who lived in the city, and then gave it as a dowry for his daughter, Solomon's wife.**" (ISV)

Jubilee Bible 2000: "**Pharaoh, king of Egypt, had gone up and taken Gezer and burnt it with fire and slain the Canaanites that dwelt in the city and given it *for* a gift unto his daughter, Solomon's wife.**" (JUB)

Authorized (King James) Version: "***For* Pharaoh king of Egypt had gone up, and taken Gezer, and burnt it with fire, and slain the Canaanites that dwelt in the city, and given it *for* a present unto his daughter, Solomon's wife.**" (AKJV)

**Day 10:** In 2 Kings 9:16 we read, **So Jehu rode in a chariot, and went to Jezreel; for Joram lay there. And Ahaziah king of Judah** [he was a wicked king, but his going to see Joram, who was recovering from battle wounds, goes to show you that all people have some good in them] **was come down to see Joram.**" (KJV)

We see three personalities here in this verse: Jehu the wild man in the chariot who would later kill Joram; Joram, who was wounded in battle; and Ahaziah, king of Judah. The writer of this verse had to say which king this was, because both the southern and northern kingdoms had a king named Ahaziah.

Second Kings 8:28–29 sets the stage for 2 Kings 9:16. My birthday verse alone leaves us with a lot of questions.

Second Kings 8:28–29 reads, **And he** [Ahaziah, the wicked king of Israel, the son of Ahab] **went with Joram the son of Ahab to the war against Hazael king of Syria in Ramothgilead; and the Syrians wounded Joram. And king Joram went back to be healed in Jezreel of the wounds which the Syrians had given him at Ramah, when he fought against Hazael, king of Syria. And Ahaziah the son of Jehoram king of Judah went down to see Joram the son of Ahab in Jezreel, because he was sick."** (KJV) King Joram went back to be healed in Jezreel of the wounds that the Arameans, the people of Aram, which king Hazael was over, had inflicted. Things were tumbling because of sin. Ahab, who set the stage for Israel to fall, was a mean, wicked, and ungodly king. He was the eighth king of Israel. He married Jezebel. Jeroboam was the first king of northern Israel against Rehoboam, son of Solomon. Baasha was the third king of northern Israel. He followed Nadad son of Jeroboam, Baasha overthrew Jeroboam's line and reigned twenty-one years. Ahab was a shady character, and with his dirty wife at his side, they were double trouble. The dogs ate Jezebel's body after two or three eunuchs threw her down from the house and Jehu trod her under his horse's feet. The two kingdoms fell hand in hand. Sin and debauchery can cause this kind of confusion. There were murders and killings—they come with sin.

Ahab died in battle from a stray arrow striking him in exactly a critical spot in his armor. Numbers 32:23 tells us, **Your sin will find you out."** (KJV) Of the twenty kings throughout two hundred eight years, not one was a good one. The southern kingdom had nineteen kings—only five of them were righteous. No wonder they went into bondage and slavery. Second Kings 9:16 contains twenty-five words; the middle one is *lay*. This verse is all about Joram and his wounds. My birthday verse starts out with Jehu riding in his chariot. Jehu was a wild man in that chariot—it says of him in verse 20 that he drove his chariot *furiously*. This is where we get the saying "You drive like Jehu," which means wildly at high speed and unsafe. You would be shocked by the many other sayings that come from the Bible that are being used today.

**Theme:** Learn from the lessons of the Israelites' history about the consequences of unfaithfulness to God and about God's patience and faithfulness. (Gateway bible)

Overview: According to the <u>King James Study Bible</u>, the books of Kings were originally one book in the Hebrew text and formed a two-volume corpus with the books of Samuel. Second Kings is actually the fourth book in the series on the history of the Hebrew kings as presently arranged. It also serves as the final account of the demise of the divided kingdoms of Israel and Judah. The narrative of this volume concentrates on the miraculous ministry of the prophet Elisha. Events parallel the prophetic ministries of Amos and Hosea in Israel and eight prophets of Judah, including Isaiah and Jeremiah. The book also covers the reigns of Amaziah (853 BC) to Hoshea (722 BC) in Israel, and the reigns of Jehoram (848 BC) to Zedekiah (586 BC) in Judah. Included are the accounts of the Assyrian conquest of the northern tribes and the deportation of Judah in the Babylonian captivity. (Gateway bible)

II Kings 3:16 **"And he said, Thus saith the Lord, Make this valley full of ditches."** (KJV)

In chapter 3:16 we see God's battle plans and chapter

nine we see King Joram wounded from battle, verse 15a tells us **"But king Joram was returned to be healed in Jezreel of the wounds which the Syrians had given him, when he fought with Hazael king of Syria."** (KJV)

Lexham English Bible: **"Jehu mounted his chariot and went to Jezreel, for Joram *was ly*ing there, and Ahaziah king of Judah had gone down to visit Joram.** (LEB)

The Message: **"Then Jehu mounted a chariot and rode to Jezreel, where Joram was in bed, resting. King Ahaziah of Judah had come down to visit Joram."** (MSG)

Living Bible: **"Then Jehu jumped into a chariot and rode to Jezreel himself to find King Joram, who was lying there wounded. (King Ahaziah of Judah was there too, for he had gone to visit him.)"** (TLB)

Modern English Version: **"Then Jehu rode in a chariot and went to Jezreel, for Joram lay there. Ahaziah king of Judah had come down to see Joram."** (MEB)

**Day 11:** First Chronicles 9:16 reads, **And Obadiah the son of Shemaiah, the son of Galal, the son of Jeduthun, and Berechiah the son of Asa, the son of Elkanah, that dwelt in the villages of the Netophathites."** (KJV) In this thirty-two-word verse, the middle two words are <u>*son of.*</u> This terminology is used five times in this verse. The books of 1 and 2 Chronicles are a narrative of events as they happened, a recorded history, telling a story that happens under each king, whether from the north side or from the left side.

This verse tells of five generations of Obadiah and is a continuation of verse 15 and so on up to verse 14 and starts with the tribe of Levites, Shemaiah. Verse 13 speaks of the work of the house of God and able men to do the work.

Let me interject something here that I learned in my Bible school days: "There is no man who can do the work of ten men—except the man who can get ten men to do the work." The Jews' ancestries or genealogy was like that of the Mormons today: they kept good records of generations of family lines. This was a line of able-bodied men who did the work in the house of the Lord. The tribe of Levites was called to do the priest's work. Like me, I was called by God to do whatever He wanted me to do. I have no godly line before me—I helped lead my mother and father to the Lord. I am what you call a first-century Christian in my family. God just reached down and hand-picked me. It's a bit like Saul, later called Paul. God appeared to him on the Damascus road. God appeared to me in the Thomson' apartment on Academy Street in Hurlock, Maryland, on a Thursday night in October 1965.

**Theme:** The law and the prophets, like the temple, are more crucial to Israel's continuing relationship with the Lord than the presence or absence of a king; the reigns of the Davidic kings themselves being testimony. (gateway bible)

**Overview:** According to the <u>King James Study Bible</u>, the books of Chronicles were originally one book in the Hebrew text. They became separated into two books by the translators of the Greek version of the Old Testament and were given a title meaning "Things Left Behind"—that is, details not included in Samuel and Kings. The Hebrew title, "Daily Matters," like the English title "Chronicles," indicates that the material in these two books recounts the most important affairs in the lives of Israel's leaders, especially the kings. Since the major thrust of the books is to trace the record of how God's people stewarded their responsibilities as heirs of the Davidic covenant, the person of David is the central focus. First Chronicles begins with a list of names that gives prominence to the Davidic line. The genealogies end with a consideration of the house of Saul, so after the account of his death the rest of the book can deal with Israel's greatest king, David. First Chronicles concludes with a summary of King David's reign. (gateway bible)

I Chronicles 3:16 "And the sons of Jehoiakim: Jeconiah his son, Zedekiah his son." (KJV) The Chronicles has to do with generosity so both 3:16 and 9:16 deals with generations.

Some versions of the bibles with I Chronicles 9:16:

Names of God Bible: **Obadiah (son of Shemaiah, grandson of Galal, and great-grandson of Jeduthun), and Berechiah (son of Asa and grandson of Elkanah, who lived in the villages belonging to the Netophathites).** (NOG)

New American Bible (Revised Edition): **"Then Jehu mounted his chariot and drove to Jezreel, where Joram lay ill and Ahaziah, king of Judah, had come to visit him."** (NABRE)

New American Standard Bible: **"Then Jehu rode in a chariot and went to Jezreel, since Joram was lying there *recovering*. And Ahaziah the king of Judah had come down to see Joram."** (NASB)

New American Standard Bible 1995: **"Then Jehu rode in a chariot and went to Jezreel, for Joram was lying there. Ahaziah king of Judah had come down to see Joram."** (NASb1995)

**Day 12:** Second Chronicles 9:16 reads, **And three hundred shields made he** [Solomon with his riches] **of**

**beaten gold: three hundred shekels of gold went to one shield. And the king put them in the house of the forest of Lebanon."** (KJV) In this thirty-one-word verse, the middle word *to* is a preposition "**to**" referring to the shield. I remember one of my English teachers, Mrs. Bartmen, gave us some various phrases to understand the meanings of different prepositions: *into* the ball, *around* the ball, *in* the ball, under the ball, *to* the ball, *with* the ball, *over* the ball, and so on. Prepositions are very important, putting emphasis on the shields of Solomon

Solomon had many houses, one for each wife he married. First Kings 11:8 tells us, **And likewise did he for all his strange wives, which burnt incense and sacrificed unto their** [his wives'] **gods.** Verse one of this chapter tells us that **king Solomon loved many strange women, together with the daughter of Pharaoh, women of the Moabites, Ammonites, Edomites, Zidonians, and Hittites-** (KJV) women who were forbidden to the Jewish men. These women took his heart away from serving the true and living God, the God of Israel. You men, Satan has a woman just for you, to do his dirty work for him. Ladies, Satan has a man to lead you astray also.

Theme: The law and the prophets, like the temple, are more crucial to Israel's continuing relationship with the Lord than the presence or absence of a king; the reigns of the Davidic kings themselves being testimony. (gateway bible)

**Overview:** According to the <u>King James Study Bible</u>, the books of Chronicles include Israel's religious institutions—the temple, priesthood, offerings, and feasts—as the essential elements of national life. In 2 Chronicles, the individual reigns of the descendants of

David are featured, from the time of Solomon until the fall of Jerusalem under Zedekiah in 586 BC. A concluding note concerning the edict of Cyrus the Great permitting the Jews to return to Jerusalem is added at the end. Throughout 1 and 2 Chronicles the emphasis is strictly on the southern kingdom of Judah, whose fortunes are viewed in light of her faithfulness to God's commandments and the institutions of Israel's religious faith. The political fate of Judah is also seen against the rising power of Babylon and Persia, although the book's major theme is that Judah is falling because of internal weaknesses brought about by her failure to remain faithful to God. (gateway bible)

II Chronicles 3:16 And he made chains, as in the oracle, and put them on the heads of the pillars; and made an hundred pomegranates, and put them on the chains.(KJV)

Both II Chronicles 3:16 and 9:16 deals with King Solomon and his riches and what he did with them.

Other bibles with II Chronicles 9:16 in them.

New Century Version: **He also made three hundred smaller shields of hammered gold, each of which contained about four pounds of gold. The king put them in the Palace of the Forest of Lebanon**. (NCV)

English Translation: "**He also made 300 small shields of hammered gold; 300 measures of gold were used for each of those shields. The king placed them in the Palace of the Lebanon Forest.**" (NET)

New International Version: "**He also made three hundred small shields of hammered gold, with three hundred shekels of gold in each shield. The king put them in the Palace of the Forest of Lebanon.**" (NIV)

New International Version – UK: "**He also made three**

**hundred small shields of hammered gold, with three hundred shekels of gold in each shield. The king put them in the Palace of the Forest of Lebanon."** (NIRV)

**Day 13:** Nehemiah 9:16 states, **``But they and our fathers dealt proudly, and hardened their necks, and hearkened not to thy commandments."** (KJV) This seventeen-word statement here is verse 16, is right in the middle of a story. To complete the story you must read verses 12–17, which refers to the Israelite's and their problems with obeying the Word of the Lord—just like us today. We tend to want our own way, which gets us into trouble every time. We just repeat the process over and over. I read the Word of the Lord to remind me of *me,* as Paul tells us of himself in Romans 7:14–24. David quotes God in the book of praises, the Psalms: **I** [Jehovah God] **am** [the great I am, as He told Moses in the wilderness—"I am that I am"] **the Lord thy God, which brought thee out of the land of Egypt: open thy mouth wide, and I will fill it. But my people would not hearken to my voice; and Israel would none of me** (81:10–11).(KJV) I, me and myself is the one that gets in the way of serving the Lord. The middle word here in this verse is *hardened,* used twice, telling us of the condition of the children of Israel and may I add, America too.

**Theme:** Nehemiah travels from Susa in Elam to Jerusalem in Judah to lead the Jews in rebuilding the city walls. (gateway bible)

**Overview:** The Babylonians conquered Judah in 586 BC. Persia conquered Babylon in 539 BC and shortly thereafter allowed the Jews to return to Jerusalem. Despite opposition, the returned exiles rebuilt the temple (see the book of Ezra). But by 445 BC the challenges of rebuilding their homeland had demoralized the Jews, and the wall of Jerusalem remained in rubble. The **King James Study Bible** says Nehemiah succeeded in having himself appointed governor of Judah with authority and resources to rebuild the city walls. He was a man of skill and daring. He first surveyed the walls at night, to avoid detection by those who might oppose the work. Then he assembled a labor force and, dividing the walls into sections, he supervised the building process. The project was completed in the remarkably short time of 52 days despite facing determined opposition: mockery; armed raids; a ruse to draw him outside the city, without doubt to murder him; blackmail; and finally, a prophet hired to foretell his death. In every case he met the challenge with courage, wisdom, and an invincible determination to complete the task for which God had called him. If you've ever faced an overwhelming task or felt inadequate to meet a challenge, you'll identify with Nehemiah. (gateway bible)

Nehemiah 3:16 **"After him repaired Nehemiah the son of Azbuk, the ruler of the half part of Bethzur, unto the place over against the sepulchres of David, and to the pool that was made, and unto the house of the mighty.** (KJV) God gave wisdom in 3:16 and 9:16 the people swelled with pride over the wisdom that God has given them.

Other versions that have Nehemiah 9:16 in them:

New King James Version: **"But they and our fathers acted proudly Hardened their necks, And did not heed Your commandments. (NKJV)**

New Life Version: **"But they, our fathers, acted with pride. They became strong-willed and would not listen to Your Words." (NLV)**

New Living Translation: **"But our ancestors were proud and stubborn, and they paid no attention to your commands."** (NLV

New Revised Standard Version, Anglicised: **"But they and our ancestors acted presumptuously and stiffened their necks and did not obey your commandments;"** (NRSVA)

New Revised Standard Version, Anglicised Catholic Edition: **"But they and our ancestors acted presumptuously and stiffened their necks and did not obey your commandments;"** (NRSVACE)

**Day 14:** Esther 9:16 **"But the other Jews that were in the king's provinces** (A-has-u-e-rus, king of E-thi-o-pa-a an hundred twenty seven provincers) **gathered themselves together, and stood for their lives, and had <u>rest from</u> their enemies,** (O the protecting hand of God) **and slew of their foes seventy and five thousand,** (The strength that the Lord gives in time of need) **but they laid not their hands on the prey,"** (KJV) (the Jews shown character here, they could took advantage here but choose to let God do what He wills) Haman's stunt failed to execute Mori De-cai and the Jews prevailed. The tables was turned and it was the Jews turn to act. Esther was a Jew and Queen of Ethi-o-pi-a. God knows who to put of His family in the right place at the right time. God knows where you are..

Theme: The book of Esther describes how the Jews of Persia are saved from certain destruction through divine providence. (gateway bible)

**Overview:** Have you ever wondered if God is really involved in the circumstances of your life? Do personal or political crises make you question God's role in human events? The **NIV Quest Study Bible** says the book of Esther, like much of the Bible, tells the story of God's involvement with his people. Unlike the rest of the Bible, however, this book shows God's work indirectly. In fact, God's name is not mentioned once, nor is there any explicit reference to God, though his influence permeates the narrative. The book demonstrates how God worked in the lives of his people, and it will encourage you to trust him to work in your life today. (gateway bible)

Other versions with Esther 9:16:

Orthodox Jewish Bible**: "But the she'ar (remainder, remnant) of the Yehudim that were in the provinces of HaMelech assembled themselves together, engaged in self defense, got relief from their oyvim,**(enemies) **slew of those hating them 75,000, but they laid not their hands on the plunder."** (OJB)

Revised Standard Version: **The Feast of Purim Inaugurated: Now the other Jews who were in the king's provinces also gathered to defend their lives, and got relief from their enemies, and slew seventy-five thousand of those who hated them; but they laid no hands on the plunder.** (RSV)

New Revised Standard Version, Anglicised Catholic Edition: "**Now the other Jews who were in the king's provinces also gathered to defend their lives, and gained relief from their enemies, and killed seventy-five thousand of those who hated them; but they laid no hands on the plunder.**" (NRSVACE)

**Day 15:** In Job 9:16 we read, **"If I had called, and he had answered me; yet would I not believe that he had**

**hearkened unto my voice."** (KJV) Job had confidence that God would listen to him. He was talking to Eliphaz the Temanite (Job 15:1), who was an Edomite, a descendant of Esau). In 16:2 Job called Eliphaz and his company "miserable comforters he called them." In verse 3 of chapter 16 Job accused Eliphaz of uttering vain words. In verse 4 he tells Eliphaz that if the situation were turned the other way, he could heap up words against Eliphaz and shake his head at *him*. What a trying chapter on Job's emotions at a time when Job needs comfort. Job's four friends contended that Job had a secret sin and needed to repent of it. They were there to help him do just that.

Job uses the word *if*. When you see this word, it is setting up an example, it is not necessarily true. Job tells Bildad that he was in good standing with the God of the universe and that if God chooses to do whatever He wants, Job knows this will *not* cause God to cut him off and no longer hear his prayers. God sometimes chooses to not answer us to train us to exercise our faith. He is here with us and chooses to let go through our trials seemingly alone, but is there all the time. Remembering the story of the footprints in the sand.

Job needed friends like I had when my first wife left me. Glenn Phillips, (I will see him in heaven one day soon) whom I went to Bible school with, came over to my house and just sat and let Bramble ramble on and on, getting it out of my system. It's human nature to see things white or black, up or down. In John 9, upon encountering a blind man, Jesus's disciples asked whose sin was responsible for his blindness—his own or his parents'. They simply saw a sin problem. Jesus told them that it was neither his parents' sin nor his, but that the works of God should be made manifest in him (the blind man). God wants us to be living sacrifices. Job was going through that same experience, being a living sacrifice. Jesus sometimes calls us to go through difficult situations to show His power. The verse I used in showing that I was saved comes into play here.

In 1 Corinthians 10:13 we read, **There hath no temptation** [trial, sin, people, or the devil] **taken you but such as is common to man** [there is nothing new under the sun]**: but God is faithful** [in times like this you can see how faithful He really is]**, who will not suffer you to be tempted above that ye are able** [God knows your breaking points]**; but will with the temptation also make a way to escape** [it never ceases to amaze me that God can do this]**, that ye may be able to bear it** (KJV) You will be stronger, better, and more complete by this trial you just went through] (emphasis added) Let us when we see brothers or sisters in places of failure go beside them and pick them up. Let us encourage them. Let us not fall into putting down or backbiting.

Job 9:16 has twenty-one words in it and the middle word is "*I*", that all-important personal pronoun. Sometimes all we can see is me, myself, and I. Job here is defending his pathway to God. God will hear me when I cry. God allows things into our lives to do a work for us that, such as in Job's case, we or our friends may not even see at the time. Job's friend was looking on the outside, they did not see God was working on the inside of Job. He needed to be patient. Today we need to be patient—God is working on us and in us. I Peter 4:12 **"Beloved, think it not strange concerning the fiery trial which is to try you, as though some strange thing happened unto you."** (KJV)

**Theme:** This wisdom book ponders the question of whether God is a God of justice in the light of life's perplexities, such as human suffering. (gateway bible)

**Overview:** Probably the oldest book in the Bible, Job is the story of a good man who endures extreme suffering and wonders why. It's an honest look at responding to life's misery. But the main point of this book is the centrality of trusting God. The **NIV Study Bible** says Job shows that true, godly wisdom is to reverently love God more than all his gifts and to trust the wise goodness of God even though his ways are often beyond the power of human wisdom to fathom. Job is a profound, but painfully practical, drama that wrestles with deep troubles and concludes that righteous sufferers must trust in, acknowledge, serve, and submit to the omniscient and omnipotent Sovereign, realizing that some suffering is the result of unseen, spiritual conflicts between the kingdom of God and the kingdom of Satan— between the power of light and the power of darkness. Even though God's people may not always understand why God acts the way he does, they should rest in the assurance of knowing he understands. (gateway bible)

Other bible versions of Job 9:16

Orthodox Jewish Bible**: "If I had summoned, and He had responded to me, yet would I not believe that He had paid heed unto my kol (voice);"** (OJB)

21ˢᵗ Century King James Version: **"If I had called and He had answered me, yet would I not believe that He had hearkened unto my voice."** (KJ21)

American Standard Version: **"If I had called, and he had answered me, Yet would I not believe that he had hearkened unto my voice."** (ARV)

Amplified Bible**: "If I called and He answered meI could not believe that He was listening to my voice."** (ABP)

Job 3:16 **"Or as an hidden untimely birth I had not been; as infants which never saw light.** (KJV) Chapter three is a very low chapter in Job's life, He had to strengthen himself by faith. Hebrews 11:1 **"Now faith is the substance of things hoped for, the evidence of things not seen"** (KJV).

**Day 16 In Psalm 9:16** we read, **The Lord is known by the judgment which he executeth** [Psalm 119:62 mentions His righteous judgments and verse 66 mentions His good judgments] **the wicked is snared in the work of his own hands. Higgaion** [a musical sign]. **Selah** [an exclamation]. (KJV)

V. 75 **I know, O Lord, that thy judgments are right, and that thou in faithfulness hast afflicted me.** (David) I Corinthians 10:13 **"There hath no temptation taken you but such as is common to man: but God is faithful, who will not suffer you to be tempted above that ye are able; but will with the temptation also make a way to escape, that ye may be able to bear it.** (KJV)

Twenty-three words occur in Psalms 9:16 <u>wicked</u> is the middle word and points to the sinners. This is a warning for the wicked to get right with God. The Psalms teach us how to praise the Lord and how to be happy. Wicked is an adjective telling us of the people who are not saved and do what is right in their own eyes.

**Theme:** The book of Psalms contains ancient Israel's favorite hymns and prayers, which were used in their worship of God, the Great King. (gateway bible)

**Overview**: the book of Psalms is a collection of 150 ancient Hebrew songs and prayers. As the <u>NIV Quest Study Bible</u> says, psalms give voice to personal feelings; they are poetry, not doctrinal essays. The psalmists frequently were interested in how something felt more than what it meant. Think of the psalms as entries in a diary; they reflect people's most intimate encounters with God. Watch for figures of speech, exaggerations, and repetitions. Poetic language requires that you read with your heart as well as your mind. The <u>NIV Cultural Backgrounds Study Bible</u> says the various psalms help us see that God responds to us in our emotional highs and lows. (gateway bible)

Amplified Bible, Classic Edition: "**The Lord has made Himself known; He executes judgment; the wicked are snared in the work of their own hands. Higgaion** [meditation]**. *Selah*** [pause, and calmly]" (ABPC)

BRG Bible**: "The Lord is known** *by* **the judgment** *which* **he executeth: the wicked is snared in the work of his own hands. Higgaion. Selah.**" (BRG)

Christian Standard Bible: "**The Lord has made himself known; he has executed justice, snaring the wickedby the work of their hands. Higgaion. *Selah*** (CSB)

Common English Bible**: "The Lord is famous for the justice he has done; it's his own doing that the wicked are trapped. *Higgayon. Selah*** (CEB)

**Day 17:** Proverbs 9:16–17 says, **Whoso is simple** [simple-minded], **let him turn in <u>hither</u>** [do not go to the doors of her house, the woman of the street]; **and as for him that wanteth understanding** [be careful where you get your understanding from]**, she saith to him,** 17 **Stolen**

**waters are sweet, and bread eaten in secret is pleasant.** (KJV) There is a lot of wrong information in a wayward woman in the Bible. Proverbs 9:16 has fifteen words; the middle word is *hither*. This word is an adverb, describing where the simple man goes who knows not that the dead are there. He is like a bird in a trap, about to be slaughtered, His days will be cut short with a ruined testimony to show for it the rest of his life. What a price to pay for a few moments of joy! Sex is always joyful, but has huge consequences. Out of the marriage unit, it is always wrong. It cost David a great deal of trouble, in his family and in his life. Joseph in Genesis was a victim of a lie that Potiphar's wife told him.

Proverbs 3:16 **"Length of days is in her** (wisdom's) **right hand; and in her left hand riches and honour."** (KJV) God is wisdom and life. In 9:16 we have an evil woman, bad advice and death. You chose which one you want?

**The theme of Proverbs is:** From daytime talk shows to advice columns and self-help books, our culture is glutted with information—but often starved for wisdom. The complexity of life requires practical counsel that is also meaningfully spiritual. Proverbs offers this spiritual depth to issues like managing money, the dangers of adultery, learning how to identify true friends, and so much more. Here you'll find wisdom that works and insights that won't wear out. As you read Proverbs, watch for contrasting issues such as foolishness and wisdom, laziness and diligence, adultery and faithfulness, and true and false friendships. Look for principles that build strong marriages, undergird faithful parenting, and establish good relationships on the job. The book of Proverbs teaches us how to be friends with God and have respect of the people around us. (gateway bible)

Other versions with Proverbs 9:16

Darby Translation: **"Whoso is simple, let him turn in hither. And to him that is void of understanding she saith.** v. 17 "**Stolen waters are sweet, and the bread of secrecy is pleasant.** (Darby)

Douay-Rheims 1899 American Edition: **"He that is a little one, let him turn to me. And to the fool she said:"** 17 **Stolen waters are sweeter, and hidden bread is more pleasant."** (DRA)

Easy-to-Read Version: **"Whoever needs instruction, come." She invites all the simple people and says,"** 17 "**Stolen water is sweet. Stolen bread tastes good**." (ERV)

Evangelical Heritage Version: **"Whoever is gullible, let him turn in here."**

**To someone who lacks sense she says,"** 17 **"Stolen water is sweet. Stolen bread tastes good."** (EHV)

Day 18: In Ecclesiastes 9:16 we read these words: Then said I,(Solomon) Wisdom is better than strength: nevertheless the poor man's wisdom is despised, and his words are not heard. (KJV) Let us try to turn this verse around without destroying its meaning. A strong man will be heard of his wisdom, but the poor-spirited man's wisdom will not be heard.

After all, Jesus said, **The poor you will always have with you** Matthew 26:11 KJV. Sometimes this verse is interpreted as if to say, "You can't overcome poverty. It's a useless cause. Don't waste your money on it." (no pun intended) To Judge a man/woman on their financial standards only, is in poor judgment on our part.

Proverbs 14:21 tells us, **He that despiseth his neighbor sinneth: but he that hath mercy on the poor, happy is**

**he.**(KJV) In James 2:1–9, 15–17 we read these words: **My brethren, have not the faith of our Lord Jesus Christ, the Lord of glory, with respect to persons. 2 For if there come unto your assembly a man with a gold ring, in goodly apparel, and there come in also a poor man in vile raiment; 3 And ye have respect to him that weareth the gay clothing, and say unto him, Sit thou here in a good place; and say to the poor, Stand thou there, or sit here under my footstool: 4 Are ye not then partial in yourselves, and are become judges of evil thoughts? 5 Hearken, my beloved brethren, Hath not God chosen the poor of this world rich in faith, and heirs of the kingdom which he hath promised to them that love him? 6 But ye have despised the poor. Do not rich men oppress you, and draw you before the judgment seats? 7 Do not they blaspheme that worthy name by the which ye are called? 8 If ye fulfill the royal law according to the scripture, Thou shalt love thy neighbor as thyself, ye do well: 9 But if ye have respect to persons, ye commit sin, and are convinced of the law as transgressors. . . . 15 If a brother or sister be naked, and destitute of daily food, 16 And one of you say unto them, Depart in peace, be ye warmed and filled; notwithstanding ye give them not those things which are needful to the body; what doth it profit? 17 Even so faith, if it hath not works, is dead, being alone.** (KJV)

Of the twenty-one words in Ecclesiastes 9:16, the middle word is *poor*. Solomon considered himself as poor in spirit. He knew how to give godly advice. Look at the Proverbs and even Ecclesiastes and also the Song of Solomon, all penned by Solomon but to follow it was not there for him. Sounds like some of us, doesn't it or someone we know.

Ecclesiastes 3:16 **"And moreover I saw under the sun the place of judgment, that wickedness was there; and the place of righteousness, that iniquity was there.** (KJV)

Wickedness and iniquities are in poor taste for anybody.

The main theme of Ecclesiastes is humanity's fruitless search for contentment. Solomon, the writer of the book, says contentment (as a state of mind) cannot be found in human endeavors or material things, while wisdom and knowledge leave too many unanswered questions. Solomon was that man void of understanding and hastening to his death because of the many strange women he had. He was a prime example of the fact that money cannot buy genuine happiness. Now Paul said in 1 Timothy 6:6, **Godliness with contentment is great gain.** (KJV) I Like to think of this as my second life verse.

**Overview:** If the deep and perplexing issues of life intrigue you, you'll appreciate Ecclesiastes. The **NIV Quest Study Bible** says this book shows how a life not centered on God is purposeless and meaningless. Ecclesiastes has lots of surprising elements you wouldn't expect to find in the Bible: honest confessions of doubts, struggles with faith, and disillusionment. The prologue (1:1–11) and an epilogue (12:9–14) frame the book's contents to reveal a proper, God-fearing attitude toward life. Watch out for isolated statements; they must be understood within the context of the whole book and, ultimately, the context of the whole Bible. The author ends with the conclusion of the matter: fear God and keep his commandments, for this is the duty of all mankind. (gateway bible)

Other version's renderings of Ecclesiastes 9:16:

English Standard Version**: "But I say that wisdom is better than might, though the poor man's wisdom is despised and his words are not heard."** (ESV)

Expanded Bible: **"I still think said that wisdom is better than strength. But ·those people forgot about the poor man's wisdom and were despised, and they stopped listening to what he said."** (EXB)

1599 Geneva Bible: **"Then said I, Better is wisdom than strength: yet the wisdom of the poor is despised, and his words are not heard."** (GNV)

GOD'S WORD Translation: **"So I said, "Wisdom is better than strength," even though that poor person's wisdom was despised, and no one listened to what he said."** (GW)

Good News Translation: **"I have always said that wisdom is better than strength, but no one thinks of the poor as wise or pays any attention to what they say."** (GNT)

Holman Christian Standard Bible: **"And I said, "Wisdom is better than strength, but the wisdom of the poor man is despised, and his words are not heeded."** (HCSB)

**Day 19:** Isaiah 9:16 reads, **For the leaders of these people cause them to err; and they that are led of them [false leaders] are destroyed.(KJV)** This verse contains nineteen words, and the middle word is *err*. This verse is about destruction because of drifting away from the leaders of wisdom to lead, causing the leaders and the followers to make wrong choices. Isaiah tells the leaders of their wrong choices even in verses 6–7. "We frequently use these verses at

Christmastime**: For unto us a child is born, unto us a son is given: and the government shall be upon his shoulder: and his name shall be called Wonderful, Counselor, The mighty God, The everlasting Father, The Prince of Peace. Of the increase of his government and peace there shall be no end, upon the throne of David, and upon his kingdom, to order it, and to establish it with judgment and with justice from henceforth even for ever. The zeal of the Lord of hosts** [Jehovah] **will perform this."** (KJV) After all this, the leaders still had problems. Sounds all too familiar today, doesn't it? The masses of people will not listen to God or His Word. What a shame! They're missing out on so much inner happiness and inner comfort and strength. Human pride is a huge enemy here. Proverbs 16:18 **"Pride goeth before destruction, and an haughty spirit before a fall."** (KJV)

The Theme of Isaiah predicts imminent judgment—but eventual restoration—for the people of Judah and Jerusalem. Do you know Christians who live double lives? Who only seems to be playing with God? The prophet Isaiah knew people who lived double lives—his fellow Israelites—and he shared God's hatred for their duplicitous compromise. In the book of Isaiah, he challenges them to shape up and love God with all their hearts and minds. They understand the two-sided nature of God's character: mercy and judgment, grace and discipline, justice and forgiveness, exile and salvation. The tension of these great paradoxes fills the pages of Isaiah's writings, demanding a resolution each reader must make: decide to commit to faith or to unbelief. (gateway bible)

Isaiah 3:16 **"Moreover the Lord saith, Because the daughters of Zion are haughty,** (proud) **and walk with** stretched forth necks and wanton eyes, (flirting) **walking and mincing as they go, and making a tinkling with their feet:** (KJV) (wicked women with on the fingers and ankles)

Isaiah 3:16 bad leaders and 9:16 the evil kept going.
Other on Isaiah 9:16

Good News Translation: **The Lord said, "Look how proud the women of Jerusalem are! They walk along with their noses in the air. They are always flirting. They take dainty little steps, and the bracelets on their ankles jingle**. (GNT)

Other versions of the bible on Isaiah 9:16:

International Standard Version: "**For those who guide this people have been leading them astray, and those who are guided by them are swallowed up.**" (ISV)

Jubilee Bible 2000**: "For the governors of this people are deceivers, and those who are governed by them *are* lost.** (JUB)

Authorized (King James) Version**: "For the leaders of this people cause *them* to err; and *they that greed* of them *are* destroyed.**" (AKJV)

Lexham English Bible**: "And the leaders of this people were misleading *them*, and those who were led *were* confused.**" (LEB)

Living Bible: "**For the leaders of his people have led them down the paths of ruin.**" (TLB)

**Day 20 In Jeremiah 9:16** we read, **I** [Jehovah God] **will scatter them** [the children of Israel] **also among heathen, whom neither they nor their fathers have known** [God has places to put disobedient people]: **and I will send a sword after them, till I have consumed them."** (KJV) God means business and will not quit until the job is done."

This verse contains twenty-eight words and the middle two are **"have known".** God will put the Jews into places not known to them—strange people, strange ways, and a strange god. God will not play around indefinitely, there is a wrecking day coming.

I get upset over the Jewish people for their disobedience, yet I can see myself through them. In my book that is coming out later, *"Three Levels and Seven Positions"* I have a position on emotion—first, second, and third levels. On the first level we have greed. On the second level we have mixed emotions part up and part down (the middle-roaders), and on the third level we have complete victorious joy and rejoicing. In this verse here in Jeremiah we have the second level of mixed emotions. In one part God will deal with the disobedient, and in the other part He will protect the God-fearing people.

**Theme:** Jeremiah, the prophet of the new covenant, predicts Judah's Babylonian exile and ultimate restoration under the Davidic Messiah.(gateway bible)

**Overview:** The prophet Jeremiah saw Israel morally disintegrating and being destroyed militarily by its enemies. He saw Babylon attack Jerusalem in 586 BC and many of its people exiled to foreign lands. According to the **NIV Quest Study Bible** Jeremiah's grim prophecies, in both poetry and prose, continually warned Judah about God's approaching judgment because of the people's constant, willful disobedience. Yet intermingled with all the dark messages were words of hope about Judah's future redemption. Watch for Jeremiah's encouragement—prophecies that are still being fulfilled today whenever sinful hearts are transformed by God. (gateway bible)

Jeremiah 3:16 **"And it shall come to pass, when ye be multiplied and increased in the land, in those days, saith the Lord, they shall say no more, The ark of the covenant of the Lord: neither shall it come to mind: neither shall they remember it; neither shall they visit it; neither shall that be done any more.** (KJV) Israel and Judah were grossly in sins, even when the Lord sent pastors to them in verse 15. Read all about it in chapter 3 of Jeremiah. Jeremiah was a weeping prophet because of the sinful conditions of his people. They seem to want to do wrong, sounds familiar doesn't it.

The message on 3:16 **"And this is what will happen: You will increase and prosper in the land. The time will come"—God's Decree!—"when no one will say any longer, 'Oh, for the good old days! Remember the Ark of the Covenant?' It won't even occur to anyone to say it—'the good old days.' The so-called good old days of the Ark are gone for good.** (MSG)

In Jeremiah 9:16 we see God.
*In Jeremiah 3:16 we see the Jews disobeying and in Jeremiah we see God's punishment for disobeying.*

Other versions Jeremiah 9:16:
New American Bible (Revised Edition)**: "Lord, in keeping with all your just deeds, let your anger and your wrath be turned away from your city Jerusalem, your holy mountain. On account of our sins and the crimes of**

our ancestors, Jerusalem and your people have become the reproach of all our neighbors." (NABE)

The Message: "**Master, you are our God, for you delivered your people from the land of Egypt in a show of power—people are still talking about it! We confess that we have sinned, that we have lived bad lives. Following the lines of what you have always done in setting things right, setting *people* right, please stop being so angry with Jerusalem, your very own city, your holy mountain. We know it's our fault that this has happened, all because of our sins and our parents' sins, and now we're an embarrassment to everyone around us. We're a blot on the neighborhood. So listen, God, to this determined prayer of your servant. Have mercy on your ruined Sanctuary. Act out of who you are, not out of what we are.**" (MSG) the message adds verses 15-17 to complete a thought.

Names of God Bible: "***Adonay,***(Elohim) **since you are very righteous, turn your anger and fury away from your city, Jerusalem, your holy mountain. Jerusalem and your people are insulted by everyone around us because of our sins and the wicked things our ancestors did.**" (NOG)

New Century Version: **Lord, you do what is right, but please do not be angry with Jerusalem, your city on your holy hill. Because of our sins and the evil things done by our ancestors, people all around insult and make fun of Jerusalem and your people.** (NCV)

**Day 21:** Daniel 9:16 contains these words: **O Lord** [Jehovah], **according to all thy righteousness, I beseech thee, let thine anger and thy fury be turned away from thy city Jerusalem, thy holy mountain: because for our**

**sins, and for the iniquities of our fathers, Jerusalem and thy people are become a reproach to all that are about us.** This verse has fifty-one words, one of my longest birthday verses. The middle word is *mountain*. Jerusalem is the city that sets on seven mountains. How interesting is that, while we pray we can have a "mountaintop" experience! We can stay on the mountain in prayer. Daniel's prayer from 9:4 to verse 19 was an interceding prayer. He had a vision when reading the scroll from Jeremiah the prophet. In verse 21 God sent Gabriel to Daniel and granted him skill and understanding. God will still do that today if we will pray and wait on Him to answer. God's people have always been able to intercede for sinners and saints in need.

**Theme:** The Most High God is sovereign over all human kingdoms.

**Overview:** The central theological theme of this book, written by the prophet Daniel, is summarized in 4:17 and 5:21: "**The Most High** (God) **is sovereign over all kingdoms on earth.**" According to the NIV Quest Study Bible, Daniel's visions always show God as triumphant. The book's literary style is historical narrative (found mainly in chs. 1–6) and apocalyptic ("revelatory") material (found mainly in chs. 7–12). The **NIV Quest Study Bible** says Daniel offers an example of a godly man who lived obediently and courageously for God while earning the admiration and respect of non-believers in a pagan culture. The book of Daniel also inspires awe as we read how God performed miraculous rescues and humbled proud kings; and how Daniel made amazing predictions that God would triumph over nations and history.

Daniel 3:16 **"Shadrach, Meshach, and Abednego, answered and said to the king, O Nebuchadnezzar, we are not careful to answer thee in this matter.**(KJV) One of the high points in the book of Daniel,

Daniel 3:16 you have the three hebrews tell the king they were going to serve the living God and Daniel 9:16 of Daniel, telling the Lord to go easy on Jerusalem

Other renderings of Daniel 9:16

**New Century Version: "Lord, you do what is right, but please do not be angry with Jerusalem, your city on your holy hill. Because of our sins and the evil things done by our ancestors, people all around insult and make fun of Jerusalem and your people."** (NCV)

New English Translation: **"O Lord, according to all your justice, please turn your raging anger away from your city Jerusalem, your holy mountain. For due to our sins and the iniquities of our ancestors, Jerusalem and your people are mocked by all our neighbors."** (NET)

New International Reader's Version: **"Lord, you saved your people before. So turn your great anger away from Jerusalem again. After all, it is your city. It's your holy mountain. You have made those who live around us think little of Jerusalem and your people. That's because we have sinned. Our people before us did evil things too."** (NIRV)

New International Reader's Version: **"Lord, you saved your people before. So turn your great anger away from Jerusalem again. After all, it is your city. It's your holy mountain. You have made those who live around us think little of Jerusalem and your people. That's because**

**we have sinned. Our people before us did evil things too."** (NIRV)

Day 22- Zechariah 9:16 reads as follows: **And the Lord their God shall save them** [Israel] **in that day as the flock of his people: for they shall be as the stones of a crown, lifted up as an ensign** [a flag] **upon his land."** (JKV) God's banner will have the Israelites on it. In the OT we see God putting them down because of their unbelief and rebellion. In the NT we see God calling back and setting on up as an ensign for His people.

This verse contains thirty-five words, the middle being *for*, which is a coordinating conjunction indicating purpose. The Jews are to be stones in a crown. The twelve foundations are the twelve tribes of the Jewish people. They will finally recognize Jesus as their King, the one they crucified.

**Theme:** The Most High God is sovereign over all human kingdoms.

**Overview:** The central theological theme of this book, written by the prophet Daniel, is summarized in 4:17 and 5:21: "The Most High (God) is sovereign over all kingdoms on earth." According to the NIV Study Bible, Daniel's visions always show God as triumphant. The book's literary style is historical narrative (found mainly in chs. 1–6) and apocalyptic ("revelatory") material (found mainly in chs. 7–12). The **NIV Quest Study Bible** says Daniel offers an example of a godly man who lived obediently and courageously for God while earning the admiration and respect of non-believers in a pagan culture. The book of Daniel also inspires awe as we read how God performed miraculous rescues and humbled proud kings; and how

Daniel made amazing predictions that God would triumph over nations and history (gateway bible)

Other translations with Zechariah 9:16:

New International Version – UK: "**The Lord their God will save his people on that day as a shepherd saves his flock. They will sparkle in his land like jewels in a crown.**" (NIVUK)

New Life Version: "**The Lord their God will save them on that day as the flock of His people. For they are like the stones of a crown, shining in His land.**" (NLV)

New Life Version: "**The Lord their God will save them on that day as the flock of His people. For they are like the stones of a crown, shining in His land.**" (NLV)

New Revised Standard Version, Anglicized: "**On that day the Lord their God will save them, for they are the flock of his people; for like the jewels of a crown they shall shine on his land.**" (NRSVA)

There you have it—the twenty-two verses from the OT of my birthday. I only hope you get as excited as I did with mine. In writing this I can honestly say that I feel ten feet tall and bulletproof!

# The Second Section

The New Testament birthday verses

I share 3:16's with my birthday verses, 3:16's is grace of God and 9:16 is the mercy of God. I like the number 16, I will explain it later.

The first seven books of the NT have my birthday verses in them. There are nine books altogether Besides the first seven, we have Hebrews and Revelations.

The number 9 (you see in Revelations 9:16, I explain it later in more detail.

There are nine fruits of the Spirit: We have:

Matthews 9:16, Jesus as King of the Jews- the Lion- the fruit of love.

Mark 9:16, Jesus as Jehovah's servant-the ox-(power)

the fruit of Joy (attitude) J-Jesus-O-Overs, Y-Yourself last

Luke 9:16, Jesus as the son of man-the man- the fruit of peace (we have a choice to live in peace or live confusion)

John 9:16, Jesus as the son of God-Eagle- the fruit of forbearance (the strength of the eagle's wings

Acts 9:16, the fruit of kindness

Romans 9:16, the fruit of goodness

I Corinthians 9:16, the fruit of faithfulness

Hebrews 9:16, the fruit of gentleness

Revelations 9:16, the fruit of self-control (temperance, tolerance)

We see in the fruit of the Spirit in 3's,

1. three upward- (love, joy and Peace-(your relationship with Him),
2. Outward- kindness, longsuffering, gentleness, (the relationship with others)

3. Inward-goodness, faithfulness, and self-control/ temperance/tolerance) your relationship with yourself).

Back to the number, number 16 is doubled from number 8 which is a symbol of spiritual purity and kindness. Paul gives 16 things about love in I Corinthians 13. There are 16 various names and titles for God. We have in the KJV some 16 letter words: covenantbreakers, evilfavouredness, lovingkindnesses, unprofitableness, fellow-prisoners, everlastingness. A number of my birthday verses has 16 words in them, see Hebrews 9:16,

Day 23-Matthews 9:16 "**No man putteth a piece of new cloth unto an old garment, for that which is put in to fill it up taketh from the garment, and the rent is made worse.**" in Egene Peterson's book the Message; has verse 9:16 this way "No man cuts up a fine silk scarf to patch old work clothes. You want fabrics that match." Jesus was answering the question of the pharisees in verse 11 of his disciples not fasting while Jesus was with them. Jesus answered them (the Pharisees) can the children fast while the bridegroom is with them? This is like taking a piece of new clothing to patch up the old. It will defeat its purpose besides it being tacky, taking new to patch up the old. Let the christians and disciples enjoy Jesus while He is here with us

Let the tear go until you have a proper replacement for that tear. Just enjoy Jesus for now is what is being taught. Young people of today cannot even relate to not having a pair of jeans without a tear or a hole in them, today this is in style. In Luke 10, We have Jesus coming into town and

Mary met him and sat at his feet and Martha, her sister, told Jesus, do you not care that Mary is here at your feet and I am alone doing the cooking for dinner. Now dinner is needful, but time now is with Jesus. Martha has a priority problem. We cannot do two things at once, So let us enjoy the best thing first. Like the clothes with a hole in them better left alone, than ending up doing the wrong thing which will be far worse. Now let me bring this home even closer. My wife and I are both in our 70's and we have animals, one dog and one cat. I told my wife, it is time to make our mark with heaven above. Social security gives you the highest 13 quarters for your monthly Social security check and this life will have an end to it, but my heavenly dividends will not have an end to it. So back to our animals, when they are gone, they are gone, Now I love my little Murphy, but he is old and blind, I will miss that little fellow.

I told my wife, Oh well it will be doggone. (yes! A little play on words)

There are 32 words in Matthews 9:16 and the middle words are "is put" This shows action, we as christians need to be active.

Other places in the NT, the term disciples of John is used. Luke 7:18-20 **"And the disciples of John shewed Him of all these things. V.19 And John calling unto him two of his disciples sent them to Jesus. Saying, Art thou He that should come? Or look we for another? v. 20 When the men were come unto Him, they said, John the Baptist hath sent us unto Thee, saying, Art thou He that should come? Or look we for another?"** (KJV)

The followers of John were anxious to hear also, they

were just making sure. Their leader, John, doubted, therefore they were doubting also, My point here is to be very careful with our lives, people are watching us and if we are not sure of ourselves, will cause some tense moments with them because of us. I will be surprised at how many people I have caused to stumble because of me letting my Spiritual guard down.

I mention in my little introduction of the NT the 9 books containing my birthday verse are as the comparison of the fruit of the Spirit. The first being love. We see the love of Jesus, He was trying to explain to the disciples of John the love that needs to be not missed. While doing one thing, we let the others go. The fruit of the Spirit shown here is love, enjoy Jesus while you can.

**Theme:** Matthew presents Jesus as the Jewish Messiah sent by God to fulfill OT prophecy. (Gateway Bible)

**Overview:** The Gospel of Matthew serves as a transition that connects the story of the Old Testament with the story of the New Testament, helping us understand how the life and teaching of Jesus built on what had come before. According to the <u>NIV Study Bible</u>, many elements in Matthew's Gospel point to a Jewish or Jewish-Christian readership; for example, Matthew has more quotations from and allusions to the Old Testament than any other New Testament author. This does not mean, however, that Matthew restricts his Gospel to Jews. He records the coming of the Magi (non-Jews) to worship the infant Jesus, as well as Jesus' statement that the "field is the world" (13:38). These and other passages show that, although Matthew's Gospel is Jewish, it has a universal outlook. (gateway bible)

Matthew 3:16 **"And Jesus, when he was baptized,**

went up straightway out of the water: and, lo, the heavens were opened unto him, and he saw the Spirit of God descending like a dove, and lighting upon him:" (KJV) When I take away from these two verses in 3:16 and 9:16 it this. Jesus was not mixing the old life with His new life, like the old patch to the new garment. In 3:16 you have Jesus reacting and in 9:16 you have christians reacting.

Now what other versions of the bible say about Matthew 9:16:

Disciples' Literal New Testament: **And no one puts *a* patch *of* unshrunk cloth on *an* old garment. For the fullness of it takes from the garment and worse tear takes place.** (DLNT)

Douay-Rheims 1899 American Edition: **And nobody putteth a piece of raw cloth unto an old garment. For it taketh away the fullness thereof from the garment, and there is made a greater rent.** Good News Translation: **"No one patches up an old coat with a piece of new cloth, for the new patch will shrink and make an even bigger hole in the coat. (GNT)**

J.B. Phillips New Testament: **"Nobody sews a patch of unshrunken cloth on to an old coat, for the patch will pull away from the coat and the hole will be worse than ever. Nor do people put new wine into old wineskins— otherwise the skins burst, the wine is split and the skins are ruined. But they put new wine into new skins and both are preserved."** (Phillips)

New Matthew Bible: **No one patches an old garment with a piece of new cloth. For then the new piece pulls away from the garment, and the tear is made greater.** (NMB)

Day 24-Mark 9:16 "**And He** (Jesus) **asked the scribes, "What question you with them?**" (KJV) These ten words are the shortest of my birthday verses. The middle two words are "Scribes/What" The Scribes were people who wrote down the scriptures. They ask Jesus many many questions, In verse 16 Jesus questioned him, Jesus already knows the answer, He just wants to know how he would respond.

Jesus knew what question they had asked His disciples was about the healing of his son who had a dumb spirit. In the verses following verse 16, we have Jesus healing the boy and told His disciples that this healing came by prayer and fast. Are you prayed up and fasted for anything lately? This power is ours if we will only obey the word of God. Jesus already knew what it was they were asking, He wanted them to tell Him what it was to teach them a spiritual lesson. Like the account in the garden of Eden in Genesis, Jesus asked Adam, Where art thou? Now Jesus knew where Adam was, Adam did not know where Adam was! How many times have you been asking a question and knew they already know the answer. I have done the same thing. Only; I wanted a more complete answer, I didn't understand what all I knew about the matter. I then come to you with my question to get your take on the subject. If they knew why I was asking, they might keep key information back and therefore muddy the waters for me even more. If I questioned them without any explanation, they would freely give me what I needed to hear. Am I making any sense here? Like being in court, you have to attack a problem or the crime from many directions to come to the proper and right conclusion.

Doing these verses is like opening up presents at

christmas time. You cannot wait until you get inside the package to see what you have.

Here in Mark's gospel was seen the fruit of the joy of the Lord, Jesus enjoys people knowing Him and His sacrifice of the cross of Calvary. He rejoices in the interest of others understanding His mission here.

**Theme:** To encourage his readers to persevere through suffering and persecution, Mark presents Jesus as the Servant-Messiah and Son of God who died as a ransom for sinners. (Gateway Bible)

**Overview:** All-news radio stations and cable news channels give highlights of all the news in the world—in 30 minutes or less. According to the <u>NIV Quest Study Bible</u>, the Gospel of Mark follows a similar fast-paced approach to introducing Jesus the Messiah, the Son of God, as it highlights the ministry, death, and resurrection of Jesus. Coming out of obscurity, this unique God-man preached, performed miracles, and encountered both great popularity and deadly opposition. It's the greatest news story of all time. The author, John Mark, was the son of a Jerusalem widow whose home was a meeting place for early believers. He most likely recorded the events as he heard them firsthand from the disciple Peter. The book's distinctly non-Jewish flavor suggests it may have been written to Gentile believers in Rome. The Roman Empire, the dominant world power at that time, had begun to persecute Christians and Mark wanted to encourage them. He portrayed Jesus as the suffering servant who came to die. More than 40 percent of Mark focuses on the anguish and sacrifice of Jesus during his final week on Earth. Mark also portrayed Jesus as the Savior of the entire world—Gentiles as well as Jews. (Gateway Bible)

Mark 3:16 **"And Simon he surnamed Peter;** (KJV) verses 14-18 completes this verse, Jesus choosing the twelve disciples. My take on these two verses in 3:16 and 9:16 is, Jesus in 3:16 chose his disciples and 9:16 He is questioning His disciples.

What other versions say about Mark 9:16:

New Matthew Bible**: And he said to the scribes, What are you disputing with them?** (NMB)

New Testament for Everyone**: What's all the fuss about?' he asked.** (NTE)

New Life Version**: Jesus asked the teachers of the Law, "What are you arguing about with them?"** (NLV)

Tree of Life Version**: He questioned them, "What are you arguing about with them?"** (TLV)

Young's Literal Translation**: And he questioned the scribes, `What dispute ye with them?** (WYC)

Day 25-Luke 9:16 "**Then He** (Jesus) **took the five loaves and the two fishes, and looking up to heaven, He blessed them and brake, and gave to the disciples to set before the multitude**." (KJV) this 30 word verse, The middle two words are "heaven/He" this is it, heaven to gain and Jesus is my aim. Now you have the five loaves. Five is the number of grace in the bible and two fishes. Two stands for unity, like the man and his wife. Jesus was careful of thanking His heavenly father for the meal they were about to enjoy.

This verse in Luke shows me the position of confidence who as Christians should have. We have the plan already in place, all we need to do is do it accordingly to the plan set out for us in the bible.

In Luke's account of 9:16 we see the fruit of peace. Jesus was careful of feeding the multitudes with bread and fish, giving them peace of mind that their tummies were filled. At the time of this writing, It is coming up on thanksgiving here in America, where our first thanksgiving was with our new american friends, the Indians, and plenty of food will be served and the peacefulness of the abundant supply of food we have here in the good old USA. Great peace on the one who was in charge there in the desert. He was the one who said the grace for the meal. The disciples just returned from a very peaceful mission trip and the day was beginning to come to a close. The disciples wanted Jesus to send the multitude away but Jesus said. "**less they faint on their way, let us feed them**". (KJV) O what compassion Jesus has on the multitudes in that desert place. He still has that compassion today.

**Theme:** Luke presents Jesus as the Messiah and Lord whose life, death and resurrection make salvation available to all people everywhere. (Gateway Bible)

**Overview:** The Gospel of Luke presents Jesus as the Messiah and Lord whose life, death and resurrection make salvation available to all people everywhere. According to the <u>NIV Study Bible</u>, Luke's writing is characterized by literary excellence, historical detail and warm, sensitive understanding of Jesus and those around him. Luke's themes include: recognition of Gentiles as well as Jews in God's plan; emphasis on prayer, especially Jesus' praying before important occasions; joy at the announcement of the gospel or "good news"; special concern for the role of women;

special interest in the poor and in issues of social justice; concern for sinners; stress on the family circle; emphasis on the Holy Spirit; inclusion of more parables than any other Gospel; and emphasis on praising God.(Gateway Bible)

The Message: **They did what he said, and soon had everyone seated. He took the five loaves and two fish, lifted his face to heaven in prayer, blessed, broke, and gave the bread and fish to the disciples to hand out to the crowd.** (MGS)

Luke 3:16 **"John answered, saying unto them all, I indeed baptize you with water; but one mightier than I cometh, the latchet of whose shoes I am not worthy to unloose: he shall baptize you with the Holy Ghost and with fire:** (KJV) My take on these two verses is in 3:16 Jesus gives us the boldness and the blessed Holy Spirit, in 9:16, Jesus feed us Spiritual food as we need it or should I say; as I want it.

What other verses of the bible are saying about Luke 9:16:

Modern English Version: **Then He took the five loaves and the two fish, and looking up to heaven, He blessed them, and broke them, and gave them to the disciples to set before the crowd.** (MEV)

The Living Bible: **Jesus took the five loaves and two fish and looked up into the sky and gave thanks; then he broke off pieces for his disciples to set before the crowd".** (TLB)

The Passion Translation: **After everyone was seated, Jesus took the five loaves and two fish, and gazing into the heavenly realm he gave thanks for the food. Then, in the presence of his disciples, he broke off pieces of bread**

**and fish, and kept giving more to each disciple to give to the crowd.** *It was multiplying before their eyes"* *(TPT)*

Day 26-John 9:16 **"Therefore said some of the Pharisees, This man is not of God, because He keepeth not the sabbath day. Others said, How can a man that is a sinner do such miracles?** (now these people are making a lot of sense) **And there was a division among them"** (KJV)

Thirty nine words in this verse, one of my longer birthday verses. The middle word is "day" The most controversial; subject was the day that Jesus healed the blind man on the sabbath day. Matthew 12:8 **"For the Son of man is Lord even of the sabbath day."** (KJV)

Hardest thing for me would be; being blind from my birth. How cruel can you get when a man who never saw, came into the square seeing and Pharisees did not rejoice with him.

The position I get from this verse is the 2nd level of emotions which is mixed, part of the people doubting and part of the people rejoicing. I get goosebumps just reading this account of this man receiving his sight for the first time in his life.

I have an eye problem and was cross eyed for the first 16 years of my life and could not walk until I was 3 before I got my glasses. At the age of sixteen I got my eyes operated on to straighten them up. After missing most of my learning years being crossed and wearing glasses. On top of bringing cross eyed and wearing glasses, I was called four eyes from my classmates because of my thick glasses.

When I was married and had two children, I saw the need to go back to school to complete what I missed in grade and high school. I entered bible school in Greenville SC at the age of 25 and finished five years later with a grade average of 87 and a THG and BA degree in bible and education. O yes! I can relate to this blind man in John chapter 9. I can also relate to cruelty of the pharisees. We do not think of the feelings of others when we make accusations like that. People with this kind of actions, I feel sorry for because they are at a low point in their life and want to drag everyone down to his/her level.

The fruit of Spirit here in John 9:16 is the fruit of patience (forbearance). This man has to have the gift of forbearance. That he is patient, self-control, restraint and tolerance. We can see this in chapter nine of John with the man dealing with pharisees. v.11 "**He** (the, use to be blind man) **answered and said, A man that is called Jesus made clay, and anointed mine eyes, and said unto me, go to the pool of Siloam and wash: and I went and washed, and I received sight.**" Verse 25 "**He answered and said, Whether He be a sinner or not. I know not: one thing I know, that whereas I was bling, now I see.**" (KJV)

Amen! to him who stood up to those men. Dealing with sinners and babies in Christ, he needed self-control and forbearance.

**Theme:** John presents Jesus as the Word, the Messiah and the incarnate Son of God, who has come to reveal the Father and bring eternal life to all who believe in him. (Gateway Bible)

**Overview:** It's clear from the first paragraphs of this Gospel that the disciple John broke sharply from the styles of the other Gospel writers—Matthew, Mark, and Luke.

They focused on events, following Jesus through the bustling marketplaces and villages. Unlike them, John assumed that readers knew the basic facts about Jesus. Instead, he mulled over the profound meaning of what Jesus had said and done. The <u>NIV Student Bible</u> says the book of John reads as if it were written under a great shade tree by an author who had lots of time for reflection. In his first sentence, John highlights Christ's nature. John's book tells the story of the eternal Word who became flesh and dwelt with humanity. People often turn to the Gospel of John because it spells out so clearly the basics of the Christian faith. Jesus proves who he is, diagnoses humanity's problems, and bluntly describes what is necessary for conversion to everlasting life. (Gateway Bible)

John 3:16 **"For God so loved the world, that he gave his only begotten Son, that whosoever believeth in him should not perish, but have everlasting life.** (KJV) I talk in length in the beginning of this book on John 3:16 but here we have the comparison of 9:16 and 3:16 which is this. God caring 3:16a Jesus loving in 3:16b and in 9:16 some people rejoicing and some people envying. what Jesus did.

Other renterings of John 9:16

American Standard Version: **Some therefore of the Pharisees said, This man is not from God, because he keepeth not the sabbath. But others said, How can a man that is a sinner do such signs? And there was a division among them.** (ASV)

American Standard Version: **Some therefore of the Pharisees said, This man is not from God, because he**

**keepeth not the sabbath. But others said, How can a man that is a sinner do such signs? And there was a division among them.** (CSV)

Common English Bible: **Some Pharisees said, "This man isn't from God, because he breaks the Sabbath law." Others said, "How can a sinner do miraculous signs like these?" So they were divided**. (CEB)

Complete Jewish Bible**: At this, some of the *P'rushim* *(Pharisees)* said, "This man is not from God, because he doesn't keep *Shabbat*." But others said, "How could a man who is a sinner do miracles like these?" And there was a split among them.** (CJB)

Day 27 Acts 9:16 **"For I** (Jesus) **will shew him** (Saul, later Paul) **how great things he must suffer for my name's sake."** (KJV) Jesus was talking to Ananias, a follower of Christ, about Saul the new convert, who was persecuting the church and God's people. The fruit of Spirit here is kindness. So the Lord showed him kindness instead of evil. Paul is not used to this kind of action. That is why he said to the Lord "why persecutest thou me" When we are guilty of something, sometimes that is all we see others doing to us. We need to get away from this kind of mindset.

This birthday verse here has 15 words in it and the middle word is "things" There are some things Saul needs to shed. In this chapter we have Saul getting saved. Losing and gaining his sight. God called him to be a choosing vessel, he escaped in a basket over a wall from harm and Barnabas took up for him to the apostles.

The position I see in this verse is "mental in the 2$^{nd}$ level". After reading this verse I have the mental conscience that God will carry me through the tough times. In Acts

9:16 we see that Paul will suffer for Christ's sake. We too will suffer for our Lord.

I Peter 4:12-13 "**Beloved, think it not strange concerning the fiery trial which is to try you, as though some strange thing happened unto you:**" (KJV) I don't care how bizarre things get, remember the God of the universe has everything under control. Now verse 13 "**But rejoice, inasmuch as you are partakers of Christ's sufferings; that, when His glory shall be revealed, you may be glad also with exceeding joy.**" (KJV) His glory shall be revealed at our homecoming. Christ suffered for us! Why don't we suffer for Christ?

II Timothy 3:12 "**Yea, and all that will live godly in Christ Jesus shall suffer persecution.**" (KJV) It doesn't seem fair in order to live closer to Jesus, you have to suffer persecutions. That is where our growth comes in and we are a bigger witness to Him because of it.

I Peter 2:19 "**For this is thankworthy, if a man/woman for conscience toward God endure Grief, suffering wrongfully.**" (KJV) Here is my word again "conscience" This is a science of confidence. People will suffer wrongfully, we need to read verses like this to handle it. We could be in the wrong at the right time, we might look like someone evil or hundreds of other reasons. People are only human and to be human, we are going to err.

Psalms 119:67 "**Before I was afflicted I went astray: but now have I kept thy word.**" (KJV) Every christian needs a good thrashing from the Lord every now and then, but it is for a reason, to keep hIs word.

Psalms 119:71 "**It is good for me that I have been**

100

**afflicted; that I learn your statutes**." (word)(KJV) Here we have the Lord driving me to the word. Ever wonder why we can pick up everything to read with no problem, but the bible becomes a challenge. Ever hear the old adage "sin will keep you from this book and this book will keep you from sin," This verse is God's way to keep you in the book and away from sin.

These verses will give you an idea on the subject of suffering. The "hows", and the "whys", how to react, how to feel while suffering. We hate pain, and suffering It brings pain to the outside or to the inside, or both. Remember God does not waste pain. There are more verses on this subject of pain and suffering that I could use here. You can study them, some keywords to use, pain, suffer, afflictions, and trials.

Paul tells us in Romans 8:17-18 "**And if children, then heirs; heirs of God, and joint-heirs with Christ; if so be that we suffer with Him, that we may be also glorified together.** V.18 "**For I reckon that the sufferings of this present time are not worthy to be compared with the glory which shall be revealed in us.**" (KJV)

The fruit here is the fruit of kindness. Here Saul, later called Paul, was on his way to persecute christians and to bring them back to be put in jail. Jesus asked Saul, (later called Paul, the name of Saul means "to pray for", the name of Paul means "small". Paul after this event on Damascus road became small in his own eyes, but big in the Lord's eyes) "**Why persecute me?**" (KJV) Jesus would show kindness to him again by sending Ananias to Saul for him to receive his sight back again. I see the kindness of Christ all through the bible. His ultimate kindness is when He died on the cross for yours and my sins. Paul an honest man, in his writings inI Timothy 1:13 "**Who** (Jesus) ("I", here is understood) "I" **was before a blasphemer, and a persecutor, and injurious:** (is an adjective, showing wicked intentions, God knew he had in his heart before the damascus road experience) **but I obtained mercy, because I did it ignorantly in unbelief."** **(KJV)**

Paul was a humble man for in the same chapter he stated that God came into the world to save sinners. "**Who I am chief."** (KJV)

God saw me as I tried to read the bible at the age 16 and he knew my heart was in the right place. So four years later when I was in my bedroom, with hell on my mind, My wife had told me that I was a sinner and would go to hell if I didn't get saved and knew I did not want to go there, I was on my knees and God saved me. You see I was a first century christian in my family. So God came to me Himself and I got saved. The God of heaven shows kindness everyday to the just and to the unjust.

**Theme:** Luke shows how the gospel spread rapidly from Jerusalem to the whole Roman Empire, and from its Jewish roots to the Gentile world. (Gateway Bible)

**Overview:** Luke wrote this book as a historian to tell what happened after the resurrection of Jesus. It's the second volume of the good news—the sequel to the Gospels. In it Luke explained Christianity's amazing growth—perhaps to legitimize the church to civil authorities or to confirm the faith of believers. The <u>NIV Quest Study Bible</u> says Luke seems to have wanted congregations to understand the source of conflict between Jewish and Gentile Christians who were brought together through Jesus the

Messiah as members of God's family. These difficulties faced by the early church can serve as an encouragement to us in the present-day church. The disciples' zeal that took the gospel across ethnic and national boundaries can also inspire us today. The Spirit so active in Acts is the same Holy Spirit that is currently at work today in the church. (Gateway Bible)

Acts 3:16 **"And his name through faith in his name hath made this man strong, whom ye see and know: yea, the faith which is by him hath given him this perfect soundness in the presence of you all.** (KJV) Jesus in His analogy of a vision, made that vision come true with the conversion of Saul, later his name changed to Paul.

Other Bible translations with Acts 9:16 in them:

Contemporary English Version: **I will show him how much he must suffer for worshiping in my name."** (CEV)

Literal New Testament: **Then some of the Pharisees were saying, "This man is not from God, because He does not keep the Sabbath". But others were saying, "How is a sinful man able to do such signs?" And there was *a* division among them.** (DLNT)

Easy-to-Read Version: **Some of the Pharisees said, "That man does not obey the law about the Sabbath day. So he is not from God." Others said, "But someone who is a sinner cannot do these miraculous signs." So they could not agree with each other.**(ERV)

Evangelical Heritage Version: **Then some of the Pharisees said, "This man is not from God because he**

**does not keep the Sabbath." Others were saying, "How can a sinful man work such miraculous signs?"** (EHV)

Day 28-Romans 9:16 **"So then it is not of him that willeth, <u>nor of</u>** (is an adjective to the word "him", you or I, who are christians) **him that runneth, but of God that showeth mercy."** (KJV) Get our eyes off of self and look to the Lord who has great grace and mercy.

"So then" in verse 16 is referring to verse 15 **"For He (Jesus) saith to Moses, I will have mercy on whom I will have mercy, and I will have compassion on whom I will have compassion"** (KJV) God is God and He can do anything He wishes to do with or with anything. Without question I will follow the Lord. Now let me stop to explain something, we can ask questions in a more informational heart, not with a heart of emotions, with an attitude. There is a big difference.

Romans 9:16 has 20 words in it and the middle two are "<u>nor of</u> " is a connector of the first part of verse 16 to the last part.

The fruit of the Spirit is goodness. I see the goodness of God through the Lord Jesus Christ in this verse to Paul.

I see my position in the Lord, my religious responsibility is to live before him in all ah and respect. With joy and praise

**Theme:** Paul writes to the church in Rome to present his basic statement of the gospel: God's plan of salvation for all peoples, Jew and Gentile alike. (Gateway Bible)

**Overview:** Romans has been called "The Constitution of Christianity," "The Christian Manifesto," and "The Cathedral of the Christian Faith." It is noteworthy for being the most complete compendium of Christian doctrine. The

<u>King James Study Bible</u> says the apostle Paul had three objectives in writing this epistle: (1) to teach the fundamental doctrine of salvation to fortify believers against their enemies; (2) to explain the unbelief of Israel and vindicate the faithfulness of God in his dealings with Israel; and (3) to give practical instruction concerning Christian living in the society of his day. The <u>NIV Quest Study Bible</u> says Romans, rich in theology and teaching, communicates the details of how a person is redeemed, transformed, sealed, and sanctified for that day when we will all stand before the Lord. It explains that salvation is received by grace through faith. It articulates the foundation of Christian belief, explaining how the good news of salvation has been made available through Jesus' death on the cross and is actualized through the Holy Spirit's work in us. (Gateway Bible)

Romans 3:16 **"Destruction and misery are in their ways: (KJV) The comparison here are the works of the sinners in 3:16 ane in Romans 9:16 the works of the christians**

Other renderings of Romans 9:16

Darby Translation: **So then [it is] not of him that wills, nor of him that runs, but of God that shews mercy.** (DARBY)

Easy-to-Read Version: **So God will choose anyone he decides to show mercy to, and his choice does not depend on what people want or try to do.** (ERV)

**Holman Christian Standard Bible: So then it does not depend on human will or effort but God who shows mercy.** (HCSB)

Jubilee Bible 2000: **So then *it is* not of him that wills, nor of him that runs, but of God that has mercy.** (JUB)

Day 29 I Corinthians 9:16 **"For though I preach the gospel. I have nothing to glory of: for necessity**(compelling) **is laid upon me; yea woe** (a warning sign) **is unto me, if I preach not the gospel!"** (KJV)

II Timothy 4:7-8 "I **have fought a good fight, I have finished my course, I have kept the faith. 8 Henceforth there is laid up for me a crown of righteousness, which the Lord, the righteous judge, shall give me at that day: and not to me only, but unto all them also that love his appearing. (KJV)**

After Paul's conversion, God planted a drive into Paul to preach the gospel. Paul goes on to say that he was not preaching he would have trouble on his hands. God has given each one a talent or a gift to be used in His service, we can find these gifts in I Corinthians 12, Romans 12, and Ephesians 4. These spiritual gifts are related to both seemingly "natural" abilities and seemingly more "miraculous" abilities, empowered by the Blessed Holy Spirit.

There are 29 words in this verse and the middle word is, "**is**" its definition is present tense third-person singular of "be"; Now in bible school in my English class I learned not only the eight parts of speech in the past, present and future tense. Not only that but what tense a person one is speaking in. Let me give an example: I-first person, My-second person and theirs-third person. Now the pronoun "you" is generic, we use that word "you" for all three persons: Past, present and future.

My position in this verse would be Spirit filled, We all

have the power of God and it is up to us, how much power will we allow in our lives from our heavenly Father. Now can I say this, we as saved individuals are like the toy yo yo, we are up and down, down and then up with this christian life. We stay more stable by reading the bible and by our prayers to God, the Father, and the Lord Jesus Christ.

Paul makes a statement in the first third of this verse. He gives two warnings in the remainder of the verse, necessity is that I must preach the gospel and woe to Paul with pain and suffering, if he did not preach. God would send trouble and heartache our way if we do not do as God wants us to do. He has or will make it clear to us, We all have a divine design. Let us use it..

**Theme:** Paul addresses problems in the church and answers questions from the church. (Gateway Bible)

**Overview:** Fights. Rumors. Factions. It's all here in 1 Corinthians. The <u>NIV Quest Study Bible</u> says few other books of Scripture reveal the human weaknesses of Christians as vividly as this book does. Some other topics include: How do you deal with a sex-crazed society? Divorce—when is it justified? Can Christians sue? Get ready! You're about to encounter God's perspective on some hot topics. You'll also read about how the church must seek unity as we learn to love one another—with all of our shortcomings. And in the process, you'll see how the church can impact today's world. The book is perhaps most popular for its chapter on love (13) and the resurrection (15). (Gateway Bible)

I Corinthians 3:16 "Know ye not that ye are the temple of God, and that the Spirit of God dwelleth in you? (KJV) I could not pick any two verses that acted on each other if I tried.

3:16 We realize that we are the temple of God and 9:16 We realize that neccessiley if I didn't preach the gospel.

Other versions of I Corinthians 9:16:

Living Bible: **For just preaching the Gospel isn't any special credit to me—I couldn't keep from preaching it if I wanted to. I would be utterly miserable. Woe unto me if I don't.** (TLB)

The Message: **Still, I want it made clear that I've never gotten anything out of this for myself, and that I'm not writing now to get something. I'd rather die than give anyone ammunition to discredit me or question my motives. If I proclaim the Message, it's not to get something out of it for myself. I'm *compelled* to do it, and doomed if I don't!** (MSG)

Modern English Version: **Though I preach the gospel, I have nothing to boast of, for the requirement is laid upon me. Yes, woe unto me if I do not preach the gospel!** (MEV)

Names of God Bible: **If I spread the Good News, I have nothing to brag about because I have an obligation to do this. How horrible it will be for me if I don't spread the Good News!** (NOG)

New American Standard Bible: **For if I preach the gospel, I have nothing to boast *about*, for I am under compulsion; for woe to me if I do not preach the gospel.** (NASB)

**Day 30**-Hebrews 9:16 **"For where a testament is, there must also of necessity be the death of the testator."** There are 16 words in this verse and the middle two words are "" **also of** Jesus paid the ultimate price for us. Eugene Peterson's book the Message has this verse this way. "**His

**death marked the transition from the old plan to the new one."** (MSG) God is talking to Ananais the prophet in this verse. In order to have the one, you got to have the other, a testament and the testator.

In my bible school days, in English class, to add "er" you add a person to the word, let me illustrate; to paint is one thing, but a painter is a person who paints. Like our verse. To have a testament, an agreement between two people, like in the legal profession, it is the law, in the man and his wife, it's a lifelong agreement. A testator is Jesus making good the testament. agreement, testament the everlasting covenant. Let me pause right here and tell you, that I am not a Calvinist. They believe God has chosen who would be saved and who would not. I believe God in heaven knows who will be saved and who will not, that is the foreknowledge of God, completely over my head. It gives me great pleasure not knowing the details. I accept this by faith. You know what Paul says about faith in Hebrews 11:1 **Now faith is the substance of things hoped for, "the evidence of things not seen."** (KJV)

The number 16 stands for love. In the bible in the OT there are the various names and titles for God specially signify His constant, never-ending love for the children of Israel. The number 16 is doubled from the number 8 which is a symbol of spiritual purity and kindness. Number 16 is strongly associated with love and its manifestations. God's love can be reached not through merely obeying the commandments physically, but also deepty spiritual believing in God. showing true love and being open to others. The spiritual meaning of God's laws and commandments should be saved and kept in the hearts of the believer. The nature of physical and spiritual intent is shown in 8+8 which is 16. It leads us to one, whole and perfect love of God. The number 24 is triple 8 which is love 3 times over. The number 24 is the 24 elders spoken of in Revelations 4:4, which 4 & 4 = 8 which is a new beginning, which I got in 1965 which was my salvation experience.

Speaking of the number 3 which is the trinity, completion. You double that number and you have 6, the number of humans, add 3 to that and you have 9, the fruit of the spirit spoken of in Galatians 5:22&23. Love, Joy, Peace, longsuffering, gentleness, goodness, faith, meekness, and temperance. Quadruple it and you have 12, a governmental number, ruling, like a king. You get the picture. You can play around with numbers in your bible and see what you come up with. Go to the biblical numerology on your smartphone or on your computers.

Best of all I was born on the 16th day of the month.

Again in my birthday verse in Hebrews 9:16 **"For where a testament is, there must also of necessity be the death of the testator."** the key words is, "necessity the death of" The first one is, it is necessary and the second one is one must die. Verse 17 **"For a testament is of force after men are dead: otherwise it is of no strength at all while the testator (Jesus) liveth."** (The power came, when he died, then the blessed Holy Spirit came) John 16:7-11 **"Nevertheless I tell you the truth; It is expedient (necessary) for you that I go away: for if I go not away, the Comforter will not come unto you. Verse 8 And when he is come. He will reprove the world of sin, and of righteousness, and of judgment:** verse 9 **Of sin. Because they believe not on me;** verse 10 **Of righteousness, because I go to my Father, and ye see**

**me no more.** verse 11 **O judgment, because the prince of this world is judged."** (Satan has already been judged)

Are we getting the picture here?

Let me word it this way, In order to have a complete testament (covenant, or an agreement) You must have a completer of that unconditional testament, one who will die to complete that covenant/agreement relationship.

Let me clear up the muddy waters here, why did I add the word unconditional, because of the word necessity. To complete the priest's duties, not an animal as in the OT, but a human as in the NT. must die. John 11:49-51 **"And one of them,** (Caiaphas, v.47a **"the named Caiaphas, being the high priest that same year, said unto them, You know nothing at all, chief priests and the pharisees"** v.50 **Nor consider that it is expedient for us, that one man should die for the people, and that the whole nation perish not.** V. 51 **And this spake he not of himself: but being high priest that year, he prophesied that Jesus should die for that nation:"** (KJV) Caiaphas was the priest that year, they switched when one was too old, 25-50. Numbers 8:24-25 **"This is it that belongeth unto the Levites: from twenty and five years old and upward they shall go in to wait upon the service of the tabernacle of the congregation:"** v.25 **"And from the age of fifty years they shall cease waiting upon the service thereof, and shall serve no more:"** Leviticus 21:13-14 **"And he shall take a wife in her virginity."** v,14 **A widow, or a divorced woman, or profane, or a harlot, these shall he not take: but he shall take a virgin of his own people to wife,"** (KJV) Just a word to this verse, people who is under the big "D" (divorce) is not limited, if you can serve, then serve, If your followers knows your saturation and still want you to hold that office, go for it. Now back to the verse that is quoting the qualification on a wife the priest, widows, divorce, profane, and a harlot. All women are in the same boat, off limits to the priest. Why!? Do we want to pick on just the divorced.

I am a divorce man, are you going to stop reading this book because of that? No! No, my brothers and sisters, God's grace is too big for us to throw stones, we have a job to do, so let us get on with it. Yes! You have verses like Romans 7:2 "**For the woman which hath an husband is bound by the the law to her husband so long as he liveth; but if the husband be dead, she is loosed from the law of her husband.**" (KJV) I inserted this verse to show that I don't want to be guilty of picking and choosing to please me. We are to teach the whole counsel of God. You can teach people not to do as we have done but this is what God teaches, we are an authority on it, because we have experienced it. I'd rather hear a divorce person teach on divorce, than a non-divorced person. I know, I was that person for 53 years, I look back on my teaching on the subject then and my teaching on divorce now, so there is no comparison. I can speak with authority now.

Caiaphas is quoting from Isaiah chapter 53, stop and read these 12 verses. Again notice the number 12, an authoritative number. Hebrews is the Leviticus of the New testament. These two books are priestly books. We see Jesus as the prophet, priest and king.

The book of Hebrews is a priestly book, a go between book. Like your modern day priest. The priest on that day was to take the sacrifices of the people and present it to God for his/her sins.

You can see why the bible is so important to me and everybody else who believes it. That the things of the bible fits in every area of our life. It has and is and forever will perform miracles for us. In my birthday verse in Leviticus was one the duties of the priest before he became the high priest. One has to pay his dues to the priest's office before he becomes the high priest.

**Theme:** The author demonstrates the absolute supremacy and sufficiency of Jesus Christ as reveler and mediator of God's grace. (Gateway Bible)

**Overview:** The theme of Hebrews is the absolute supremacy and sufficiency of Jesus Christ as revealer and mediator of God's grace. According to the <u>NIV Study Bible</u>, the prologue presents Christ as God's full and final revelation, far surpassing the revelation given in the Old Testament. The prophecies and promises of the Old Testament are fulfilled in the "new covenant" (or "new testament"), of which Christ is the mediator. From the Old Testament itself, Christ is shown to be superior to the ancient prophets, to angels, to Moses (the mediator of the former covenant) and to Aaron and his priestly descendants. Hebrews could be called "the book of better things" since the two Greek words for "better" and "superior" occur 15 times in the letter. Readers are told that there can be no turning back to or continuation of the old Jewish system, which has been superseded by the unique priesthood of Christ. God's people must now look only to him, whose atoning death, resurrection, and ascension have opened the way into the true, heavenly sanctuary of God's presence. (Gateway Bible)

Hebrews 3:16 "**For some, when they had heard,**

**did provoke: howbeit not all that came out of Egypt by Moses.**(KJV) This verse sounds like that other people around them join up with the children of Israel and they provoke the Lord and therefore make the children of God do the same thing. Wherefore in 9:16 we need to let God do His work, because He only knows what is in the heart of a person. We as christians need to be very careful who we hang out with. Remember a lot of times we are who we are by the company we kept.

Other renderings of Hebrews 9:16

New English Translation: **For where there is a will, the death of the one who made it must be proven.** (NET)

New Century Version: **So God will choose the one to whom he decides to show mercy; his choice does not depend on what people want or try to do.** (NCV)

New English Translation: **So then, it does not depend on human desire or exertion, but on God who shows mercy.** (NET)

New International Version: **It does not, therefore, depend on human desire or effort, but on God's mercy.** (NIV)

New Living Translation: **So it is God who decides to show mercy. We can neither choose it nor work for it.** (NLT)

**Day 31-** My last birthday verse, but not by no means the least, is in Revelations 9:16 **"And the number of the army of the horsemen were two hundred thousand thousand: and I heard the number of them"** (KJV) There are 21 words in this verse and the middle number is "hundred" this verse deals with numbers. This verse signifies that there are 200,000,000, yes 200 Million soldiers. That is almost ⅔ of the USA. We have as of 2020, 331,002,651 people living in America.

Verse 13 is the key to verse 16. You have 4 angels loosed, which were prepared for war for 1 year and 1 month and one day, to slay ⅓ of the men on the earth. This battle lasted for 391 days. You have 3 the trinity, 9-the fruit of the Spirit and 1- the supreme Lord Jesus Christ. You see how this all worked out. You have the Father, the Son and the Holy Spirit. I can't say this enough, that is, when it comes to the bible numbers, they just fit. When I was younger, I spent hours with problems that I made up, just working with numbers. Numbers are so important to God that He gave us a book called the Numbers.

This verse is the fruit of self-control. Self-control in all areas of your life. Take your mouth for instance, the bible has a lot to say about the tongue, bring busy bodies, gossipers. He gives us a whole chapter on the tongue in James chapter three.

This verse has twenty-one words in it and the middle word is two, I have two natures, the old of sin and the new of the Spirit. Two places, heaven or hell, two leaders, Satan or Christ. Two choices, two ways, the right and the wrong.

The broad way and the narrow way. The list goes on and on, have fun with the way you should go.

This book (bible) hits every area of life, just maybe that is why people don't like reading it. We just don't like to be wrong or read a book that tells us that we are wrong. You have two ears and one mouth, listen twice as much as you speak.

This verse fits my financial *position of the 7 position I will mention in my next book,* it talks of numbers, (money, over

115

2,000 verses in the bible) I like money just like any other person, I try to stay away from the "love" of it though, that is greed, the first level of the position of financial. Money is just a source of getting the things that you need and paying your bills.

This is the ninth birthday verse of the NT. And September being the ninth month. I can see me in this verse. With the numbers, and with the temperament of self-control.

**Theme:** John writes to encourage the faithful to stand firm against persecution and compromise in the light of the imminent return of Christ to deliver the righteous and judge the wicked.(Gateway Bible)

**Overview:** Revelation is a book of hope; its central message is that God and good will win over evil, no matter how bad things look now. Its author, the apostle John, encourages his readers to live a committed, holy life in order to participate in God's victorious kingdom. The NIV Quest Study Bible says the book was written to seven churches in the Roman province of Asia (present-day Turkey) to warn them against falling away from their faith in Christ. It also offered assurance of ultimate victory to those who remain on God's side. Revelation is apocalyptic literature. The Greek word apocalypse means "uncovering," "unveiling," or "revelation." Jewish apocalyptic writing uses figurative language and symbolism to show that evil will be replaced by the goodness and peace of God's kingdom. As you read, look for a combination of warnings and encouragements, challenge, and hope. Watch for descriptions of the future, as God's kingdom ultimately conquers evil in the last days.

Also notice the picture of the ruling Christ, his divine attributes, and his heavenly glory. (Gateway Bible)

Revelations 3:16 **"So then because thou art lukewarm, and neither cold nor hot, I will spue thee out of my mouth.** (KJV) My take of these two passages is 3:16 have loose living while God will fight our battles for us in 9:16

Other passages that has Revelations 9:16:

New Matthew Bible: **And the number of horsemen of war was twenty times ten thousand. And I heard the number of them.** LNMB)

New Testament for Everyone**: The number of the troops and horsemen was two hundred million. (I heard the number.)** (NTE)

Wycliffe Bible: **And the number of the host of horsemen *was* twenty thousand times ten thousand. And I heard the number of them.** (WYC)

Young's Literal Translation**: and the number of the forces of the horsemen [is] two myriads of myriads, and I heard the number of them**. (YLT)

Now you have my 31 birthday verses. I hope you enjoyed these verses as much as I did in typing them. I hope you start to do the same for your birthday verses in the bible. This will make your birthdays even more special and the bible more personal.

God bless!

# The Third Section

My daily bible reading verses for the day, in the quotations you find. () number of vs., T- Total of verses for that day For example Matt. For Matthew 5-7 (111) At the end total of verses ?? of that day. See Day one for example:

John 3:7 "**Do not be amazed or overwhelmed by what I said to you, You <u>must</u> be born again.**" (KJV) John 6:44a "**No one can come to me unless the Father who sent Me** (Jesus) <u>**draws**</u> **him/her** (the sinner).." (KJV) We **Must** be **drawn** and we **Must** be willing to be saved. This is imperative to understand this book.(the Bible) and they are drawn by seeing us praising God,(being the salt, we ought) and as we glow for Him. (being the light) **Stand still**, **watch**, see Him working in your Life, **Wait**, for the blessings, they are on the way. "**Blessed is he/she that <u>readeth,</u> this prophecy** (the word of God, **and keep those things which are written therein: for the time is at hand.**" (KJV) (time: of the things written in the bible, or our life here on earth) Revelation 1:3

John 5:39 "**Search the scriptures** (Jesus speaking to the unbelieving Jews) **for in them ye think** (a Hippocrates think Not! My friend, you Must know the way and that way is the way of the cross) **ye have eternal life: and they** (the words of the bible) **which testify of me.**" (KJV)(Jesus)

Psalm 119:97 David is speaking of God's word "**O how <u>love</u> I thy law! It is my meditation** (KJV) This word is on my heart and mind all the time.

I read the psalms, proverbs, the gospels and all the books 6 chs. and under once per month and the rest of the bible, the other 33 books, once per year. The Psalms teach us how to praise the Lord and how to be happy. Proverbs are for wisdom for our lives, and the gospels are godly examples from the Master Himself. The short books are how to cope in this life. (the do's and don't of life, external (actions) and internal (emotions))

Fall in love with the word and you will see such a transformation take place in your life, much more than seem possible. Only the God of the universe could do this

Psalms, all of the 2,461 verses into 5 Books: book one you have chs. 1-40, book two you have you have chs. 41-72, books 3 you have chs. 73-89, book 4 you have chs. 90-106, and book 5 you have chs.-107-150, Proverbs with 31 chs. & 915 verses the 4 Gospels with 89 chs.& 3,779 verses and the 27 short books with 81 chs & 1992 vs. Average verses per day, 307 vs.X30=9,150 vs. per month The other 33 books per year you will t-total, Example take the total of the day and the total month and day = a grand total for that day. See day 1 for example.

Psalm 117 is the shortest chapter in the bible with 2 verse ch. 118 is the center chapter of the bible w/29 vs. Psalms 119 is the longest chapter of the Bible with 176 verses.

Proverbs- a chapter per day will keep Satan at bay.

A few more facts about the bible, 2$^{nd}$ John is the shortest book w/13 vs. Esther 8:9 is the longest verse w/80 words, and John 3:35 shortest verse with 2 words

**"Jesus wep**t" (KJV)

There are 31,102 verses in the 66 books, 1,189 chapters, 260 in the New & 929 chapters in the OT in the (KJV) Bible, John 3:30 is my life verse "He **must** increase and I **must** decrease." (KJV) At Calvary, it is my life's song. If I am allowed a second choice; it would be I Timothy 6:6 "Godliness with contentment is great gain" (KJV) and my song "I can't even walk without Him holding to my hand"

John 3:7 says you **must** be born again." There are 500 verses on faith, 500 verses on love but 2,000 verses on money, 1 Timothy 6:10a "For the **Love** of money is the root of all sorts of evil" covetousness and greed are two great sins and of course the rejection of Jesus Christ.

Matthew: we see Christ as the King of the Jews (28) Chs/w1,071 vs.

Mark: we see Christ as the Servant of Man (16) Chs. with 678 vs.

Luke: we see Christ as the Servant of God (24) Chs./ with 1151 vs.

John: we see Jesus as the Savior of the World (21) Chs./ with 879 vs.

The four gospels- totals 89 chapters with 3,779 verses books under 6 chapters, there are in the OT-10 books, 31 Chapters,630 verses and in the NT-17 books- 63 chapters & 1,362 verses total 1,992 verses Ave. Bible reading total of 9,131= 304.35 verses daily, could turn your life around into pure heavenlies. and the rest of the bible (33 books) once per year 21,945 vs. divide by 360= 61 vs. per day, total of 365 vs. per day. On March 1$^{st}$ to the 4$^{th}$ of March, make up the days of 29 and 30$^{th}$ of Feb. Which will be Numbers 4-9

Why do I read this amount of the bible everyday, I am glad that you asked. In Proverbs 3:16, that I will have: "**Long life is in her right hand**; (wisdom and understanding v.14) **and her left hand are riches and honor.**" (KJV)

These bible readings will keep the Doctors and Satan at bay, you on solid ground. and on the Rock, will make you feel 10 foot high & bullet proof. It will differently personalize the bible in your life, making it a part of you.

Learn to count you bible, let me give you an example:

John 3:16 has 25 words in it, 12,12, and 1 The first 12 represents the OT and all that God the father has done.

the second 12 represents the NT and all Jesus has done

The one word represents Jesus (Son) and all he has done on the cross. The first 12 looks forward to the cross and the last 12 looks back at the cross.

We have not only the Trinity in Heaven, but we have the Word here on the earth. John 1:1 "In the beginning was the <u>Word,</u> and the <u>Word</u> was with God and the <u>Word</u> was God" v.14a "And the <u>Word</u> was made flesh, and dwelt among us." and I John 1:1 "**That which was from the beginning, which we have heard, which we have seen with our eyes, which we have looked upon, and our hands have handled, of the <u>Word of life.</u>**" (KJV) 5 times is the Word mentioned in these 3 verses, 5 means grace

My Birthday Verses, there are 31 of them. I have put one birthday verse per day with

my bible readings. My daily readings will go like this:

Example day 1 you will read chapters 1-4 of Matthews, consist of 90 verses psalms chapters 1-8 with 82 verses and Ruth chapters 1-4 with 85 verses, Proverbs chapter 1 with 33 verses with a total of 290 verses and than stroll down and after my birthday verse to January, and each month you will do the same, but on January one your will read Genesis chapter 1& 2 consisting of 56 verses and the total of 290 and 56 gives you a grand total of 346 verses for that day. Look at 2 or 3 day and you will get the picture.

**Day 1**- book 1 chs. Ps.1-8, (82) Prov.1 (33) Ruth chs. 1-4 (85) Matt. chs. 1-4 (90) = (290)

Genesis 9:16 "**And the bow shall be in the cloud; and I will l look upon it, that I <u>may</u>** (adverb to remember) **remember** (this what makes heaven, heaven and hell, hell) **everlasting covenant** (an everlasting agreement) **between God and every living creature of all flesh that is upon the earth,**" (KJV) God is no respecter of persons.

**Jan**. Gen.1-2= (56)= T(346) **Feb,** *Ex.13-14*=(53)=T(343) **Mar**. Nu. 10-12=(87)=T(377) **April**, Jos. 1-3=(59)=T(349) **May** II Sam 1-2= (59)=T(349) **June** II Ki. 17-18 =(78)=T(368) **July** 11 Chr. 34-36 (83)= T(373) **Aug**. Ecc. 7-9= (64)= T(354) **Sept** Isa. 55-56= (25)=T(315 **Oct.** Eze. 7-9 =(56)= T(346) **Nov**. Hos.13-14= (25)=T(315) **Dec**. Rom, 11-13= (71=) T(361)

**Day 2**- Ps. 9-16 (82) Prov. 2 (22) Lam 1-3:33 (77) Matt. 5-7(111)=(292)

Exodus 9:16 "**And in very deed for this cause have I raised thee up, for to <u>shew in </u>thee** (Moses) **my power, and that my name** (there is just something about that name) **may be declared throughout all the earth.**" (KJV)

Jan. Gen.3-4 (50)=T (342) **Feb** Ex.15-16=(63)=T(355) **March** Nu. 13-14=(78)=T(370 **April** Jos. 4-6=(66)=T(358) **May** II Sam. 3-4=(51)=T(353) **June** II Kings 19-20=(58)= T(350) **July** Ezra 1-2=(81)=T(373) **Aug.** Ecc.10-12=(44)=T (336) **Sept. I**sa. 57-58= (35)=T(327) **Oct.** Eze 10-12= (75)=T(367) **Nov.** Amos 1-3=(46)=T=(338) **Dec.** Ro m. 14-16= (83)=T(375)

**Day 3** Ps. 17-20=(88) Prov. 3=(35) Lam. 3:34-5:22 (77) Matt. 8-10=(114)=T(315)

Leviticus 9:16 "**Ahd he** (the high Priest/NT Jesus)

**brought the burnt offering** (Himself)**, and offered it according to the manner**." (KJV) There is an order to follow, and a command to heed.

**Jan** Gen.5-6 (54)=T(368) **Feb**. Ex17-18 (43)=T(357) Mar. Nu. 15-16=(91)=T(405) **April** Jos.7-9=(88)=T=(402) **May** II Sam. 5-6=(48)=T(362) **June** II kings 21-22=(46)=T(360) **July** Ezra 3-4=(37)=T(352) **Aug.** SS. 1-3=(45)=T(360) **Sept.** Isa 59-60=(36)=T(350) **Oct..** Eze. 13-14=(46)=T(361) **Nov.** Amos 4-6=(54)=T(369) **Dec.** Cor. 1-3=(70)=T(385)

**Day 4** Ps. 21-25=(82) Prov. 4=(27) Joel 1-3-(73) Matt. 11-13=(138)=T(320)

Numbers 9:16 "**So it was alway.**(repeat of verse 15) **The cloud covered it by day, and the appearanc**e (not fire, but as through fire) **of fire by night.**" (KJV)

Jan Gen 7-8 (46)=T(366) **Fed.** Ex. 19-20 (51)=T(371) **March** Nu, 17-18=(45)=T(365) **April** Jos. 10-12=(90)=T(410) **May** II Sam.7-8=(47)=(367) **June.** II kings 23-25=(87)=T(407) **July** Ezra 5-7=(67)=T(387)) **Aug.** SS. 4-6=(45)=T(365) **Sept.** Isa. 61-62=(23)=T(343) **Oct** Eze. 15-16=(71)=T(391) Nov. Amos 7-9=(46)=T(366) **Dec.** I Cor. 4-6=(54)=T(374)

**Day 5** Ps. 26-31=(82) Prov. 5=(23) Obad.1 & Jonah 1-2=(48) Matt. 14-16=(103)=T(256)

Deuteronomy 9:16 "And **I** (Moses) **looked, and. behold, you had sinned against the LORD, your God, and had made you** (The Jews) **a molten_calf: you had turned aside quickly out of the way which the LORD had commanded you.**" (KJV)

**Jan**.Gen.9-10 (61)=T(317) **Fed.** Ex. 21-22 (67)=T(323) **Mar.** Nu, 19-20=(51)=T(307) **April** Jos. 13-15=(111)=T(367) **May** II Sam. 9-10=(32)=T(288) **June** I Chr. 1-2=(109)=T(365) **July** Ezra 8-10=(95)=T(351) **Aug.** SS. 7-8=(27)=T(283) **Sept.**

Isa. 63-64=(31)=T(287) **Oct.** Eze. 17-18=(56)=T(312) **Nov.** Micah 1-4=(54)=T(310 **Dec.** I Cor.7-9=(80)=T(33)

**Day 6** Ps. 32-36 (95) Prov. 6=((35) Jonah 3-4=(21) Matt. 17-19=(92)=T(243)

Joshua 9:16 **"And it came to pass at the end of three days after they** (Joshua and the Jewish leaders) **had make a league** (agreement) **with them,** (Hivites v.6 & they lied v.9) **that they heard that they were their neighbors, and that they dwelt among them,"** (KJV) Take everything to God in prayer, will save us a ton of troubles and add years of peace to our lives.

**Jan**. Gen. 11-12 (52)=T (295) **Feb.** Ex. 23-24 =(51)= T(294) **Mar.** Nu. 21-22=(76=T(319) **April** Jos 16-18=(56)=T(299) **May** II Sam. 11-12=(58)=T(301) **June** I Chr.3-4=(67) =T (310) **July** Neh. 1-3=(63)=T(306) **Aug**. Isa. 1-3=(79)=T(322) **Sept** Isa.65-66=(49) =T29 **Oct.** Eze. 19-20=(63)=T(306) **Nov.** Micah 5-7=(51)-T(294) **Dec.** I Cor.1012=(98)=T(341

**Day 7** Ps.37-41=(105) Prov.7=(27) Nahum 1-3=(47) Matt 20-22=(126)=T(305)

Judges 9:16 **"Now therefore, if** (a condition) **you** (speaking to the Jewish Nation) **have done truly and sincerely,** (the bramble briers of v.15 (talking) **in that you have made Abimelech king** (a bad Philistine king) **and if ye have dealt well with Jerubbaal** (a name given to Gideon, Abimelech's father) **and his house, and have done unto him according to the deserving** (his commands) **of his hands."** (KJV) (strenuous commends)

**Jan**.Gen.13-14=(42)=T 347) **Feb.** Ex.25-26=(77)=T382) **Mar**. Nu. 23-24=(55)=T(360) **April**Jos.19-21=105=T(465) **May** II Sam. 13-14=(72)= T(377) **June** IChr.5-6 (107)=T(412)

**July** Neh. 4-6=(61)=T (366) **Aug.** Isa. 4-6=(49)=T(354) **Sept** Jere.1-3(91) =T(396) **Oct.** Eze. 21-22=(63)=T(368) **Nov.** miss readings **Dec.** I Cor. 13-14=(53)=T(358)

**Day 8** Book 2 Ps.42-48=(93) Prov. 8=(36) Habakkuk.1-3=(56) Matt. 23-25=(136)=T(321)

I Samuel 9:16 "**To morrow about this time I** (Jehovah, God) **will send thee a man out of the land of Benjamin, and thou shalt anoint him** (Saul) **to be captain over my <u>people</u> Israel, that he may save my people out of the hand of the Philistines;** (the only thing he did right) **for I have looked upon my people, because their cry is come unto me.**" (KJV) God answers Prayers for His people. God is waiting to bless us.

Three times the little phrase "my people" is mentioned. God is in the people business.

**Jan.** Gen.15-16=(37) =T (358) **Feb.** Ex. 27-28= (54)= T (375) **March** Nu. 25-26=(83)=T(404) **April** Jos. 22-24= (83)=T(404) **May** II Sam. 15-16=(60)=T(381) **June** I Chr. 7-8=(80)=T(401) **July** Neh. 7-8=(91)=T(412) **Aug**. Isa. 7-9=(68)=T(389) **Sept**. Jere. 4-6=(92)=T(411) **Oct**. Eze 23-24=(76)=T(397) **Nov**. Zec. 1-3=(53)=T(374) **Dec.** I Cor. 15-16=(82)=T(403)

**Day 9** Ps 49-54=(84) Prov. 9=(18) Zep 1-3=(53) Matt. 26-28=(161)=T (316)

I Kings 9:16 "**For Pharaoh king of Egypt had gone up and taken Gezer, and burnt it with fire, and <u>slain the</u> canaanites** (modern day Lebanese) **that dwelt in the city, and given it for a present unto his daughter, Solomon's wife.**" (KJV) (Solomon married into idolatry, who served strange gods) God warned against mixed marriages Deuteronomy 7:3 "**Neither shalt thou make marriages**

**with them; thy daughter thou shalt not give unto his son, nor his daughter shalt thou take unto thy son.**" (KJV) This verse here is extra special because it is the nine book, See day sixteen.

**Jan.** Gen.17-18(60) T (376) **Feb.** Ex. 29-30(84)=T (400) **March** Nu. 27-28=(54)=T(370) **April** Jud. 1-3=(90)=T(406) **May** II Sam. 17-18=(62)=T(378) **June** I Chr. 9-10=(58)=T(374) **July** Neh 9-11=(113)=t(429) **Aug.** Isa.10-12=(56)=T(372) **Sept** Jere. 7-9=(82)=T(398) **Oct.** Eze. 25-26=(38)=T(354) **Nov.** Zec. 4-6=(40)=T(356) **Dec.** II Cor.1-3=(59)=T(375)

**Day 10** Ps. 55-60=(87) Prov. 10=(32) Haggai 1-2 (38) Mark 1-3=(108)=T(265)

II Kings 9:16 "**So Jehu rode in a chariot, and went to Jezmreel; for <u>Joram lay</u> there, And Ahaziah king of Judah came down to see Joram.**" (KJV)

**Jan.** Gen. 19-20=(56)=T(321) **Feb.** Ex. 31-32 (53)=T(318) **Mar.** Nu. 29-30=(56)=T(321) **April** Jud.4-6= (95)= (360) **May** II Sam. 21-22=(73)=T(338) **June** I chron. 11-12 (87)=T(352) **July** Es.1-3=(60)=t(325) **Aug.** Isa.13-14=(54)=T(319) **Sept.** Jere. 13-15=(70)=T(335) **Oct.** Eze. 27-28=(62)=T(327) **Nov.** Zec. 7-9 (54)=(T(319) **Dec.** II Cor. 4-6=(57)=T(422)

**Day 11** Ps. 61-67=(81) Prov. 11= (31) Mal. 1-4= (55) Mark 4-6= (140)=T(307) I Chronicles 9:16 "**And Obadiah the son of Shemaiah, the son of Galal, the son of Jeduthun, and Berechiah <u>the son</u> of Asa, the son of Elkanah, that dwelt in the villages of the Netophathites.**" (KJV) son of repeated 5 times

**Jan.** Gen. 21-22=(58)=T(365) **Feb.** Ex. 33-34=(58)=T(365) **March** Nu,31-32=(96)=T(403) **Apr.** Jud.

7-9=(117)=T(424) **May** catch up **June** I Chron.13-14=(31) T(338) **July** catch up **Aug.** Is. 15-16=(23)=T(330). **Sept.** catch up **Oct.**Eze.29-30=(47)=T(355) **Nov.** Zec. 10-12= (43)=T(350) **Dec.** II Corin. 7-9=(55)=T(362)

**Day 12** Ps 68-69=(71) Prov.12=(28) Gal. 1-3=(74) Mark 7-9=(125)=T(298)

II Chronicles 9:16 "**And three hundred shields made he** (Solomon) **of beaten gold, three hundred shekels of gold went to one shield. And the king** (Solomon) **put them in the house of the forest of Lebanon."** (KJV)

**Jan.** Gen. 23-24 (87) =T385 **Feb.** Ex. 35-36=(73)=T(371) **March** Nu. 33-34=(85)=T(383) **April** Jud. 10-12=(73)=T(371) **May** II Sam. 23-24=(64)=T(362) **June** I Chr.15-17 (99)=T(397) **July** Es.4-6=(45)=T(343) **Aug.** Isa. 17-18=(21)=T(319) **Sept.** Jere. 16-18=(71)=T(369) **Oct.** Eze. 31-32=(50)=T(348) **Nov.** Zec.13-14=(30)=T(328) **Dec.** II Cor. 10-11=(51)=T(349)

**Day 13** Ps.70-72=(49) Prov.13=(25) Gal 4-6=(75) Mark 10-13=(166)=T(315)

Nehemiah 9:16 "**But they** (the Jewish nation **and our fathers** (our family line) **dealt proudly, and hardened their necks, and hearkened not to thy** (God's) **commandments."** (KJV)

**Jan**.Gen 25-26=(69)=T(357)) **Feb**. Ex. 37-38=(60)=T(348) **March** Nu. 35-36=(47)=T(335) **April** Jud. 13-15=(64)=T(352) **May** I Kings 1-2=(99)=T(387) **June** I Chr. 18-21 (74)=T(389) **July** Es. 7-8=(27)=T(315) **Aug.** Isa. 19-20=(31)=T(319) **Sept.** Jere. 19-22=(77)=T(365) **Oct.** Eze 33-34=(64)=T(352) **Nov.** Acts 1-2=(73)=T(361) **Dec.** II Cor. 12-13=(35)=T(327)

Day 14 Book 3 Ps. 73-76={73) Prov. 14=(35) Eph. 1-3=(66) Mark 14-16=(139)=T(313)

Esther 9:16 **"But the other Jews that were in the king's provinces gathered themselves together, and stood for their lives, and had rest from their enemies, and slew of their foes seventy and five thousand, but they laid not their hands on the prey,"** (KJV)

**Jan.** Gen. 27-28=(68)=T(381) **Feb.** Ex. 39-40=T(81)=T(39) **March** Deut. 1-2=(83)=T(396) **April** Jud. 16--18=(76)=T(389) **May** I Kings 3-4=(62)=T(375) **June** I Chr 22-24 (82)=T(395) **July** Es. 9-10=(35)=T(348) **Aug.** Isa. 21-22=(42)=T(355) **Sept.** Jere. 23-24=(50)=T(363) **Oct.** Eze. 35-36=(53)=T(366) **Nov.** Acts 3-4=(63)=T(376) **Dec.** Heb. 1-2=(32)=T(345)

**Day 15** Ps.77-78=(92) Prov.15=(33) Eph.4-6=(89) Luke 1-3=(170)=T(385)

Job 9:16 **"If I** (Job) **had called, and He** (God) **had answered me; yet <u>would</u> I not believe that he** (God) **had hearkened** (listen) **unto my voice."** (KJV) Job speaking to Bildad the Shuhite, on God's ways towards us. just that God chooses sometimes to keep silent and we have to exercise our faith.

**Jan.**Gen. 29-30=(78)=T(463) **Feb.** Lev. 1-3=(50)=T(435) **March** Deut. 3-4=(78)=T(463) **April Jud.**19-21=(103)=T(488) **May** I Kings 5-6=(56)=T(441) **June** I Chr. 25-26 (63)=T(448) **July** Job 1-3=(61)=T(446) **Aug.** Isa. 23-24=(41)=T(426) **Sept.** Jere. 25-26=(62)=T(447) **Oct.** Eze. 37-38=(51)=T(36) **Nov.** Acts 5-6=(57)=T(442) **Dec.** Heb. 3-4=(35)=T(420)

**Day 16** Ps.79-85=(99) Prov.16=(33) Phi.1-4=(104) Luke 4-6=(132)=(368)

Psalms 9:16 **"The LORD** (all caps means Yahweh) **is known by the judgment which He executeth:** (Psalms

119:62 is the righteous judgments and verse 66 the good judgements of God) <u>the</u> **wicked is snared in the work of his own hands.** (we don't have to look far to see our problems, just look into the morrow) **Higgaion,** (here it is a musical sign) **Selah."** (KJV) (and exclamation, to be set apart") I like to think of verse special because of the sixteenth day

**Jan**. Gen.31-32=(87)=T(455) **Feb**. Lev. 4-5=(54)=T(422) **March** Deut. 5-6=(58)=T (426) **April** I Sam. 1-2=(64)=T (432) **May** I kings 7-8=(117)=T(485') **June** I Chr. 27-29 (83)=T451 **July** Job 4-6=(78) =T(446) **Aug.** Isa. 25-26=(33)=T(401) **Sept.** Jere. 27-28=(39)=T (407) **Oct.** Eze. 39-40=(78)=T(456) **Nov.** Acts 7-8=(100)=T(468) **Dec.** Heb. 5-6=(34)=T(402)

**Day 17** Ps.86-89= (94) Prov. 17=(28) Col.1-4=(95) Luke 7-9=(168)=T(385)

Proverbs 9:16 "**Whoso is simple,** (minded) **let him turn in hither: and <u>as</u> for him that wanteth understanding, she** (the women of the street) **saith to him."** (KJV)

not just because of its contents, but sex is always a problem with some men. This is a warning to us.

**Jan**.Gen. 33-34=(51) T(436) **Feb**. Lev. 6-7=(68)=T(453) **March** Deut. 7-8=(46)=T(431) **April** I Sam. 3-4=(43)=T(428) **May** I Kings 9-10=(57)=T(442) **June** II Chr. 1-3=(52)=T(437) **July** Job 7-9=(78)=T(463) **Aug.**Isa.. 27-28=(42)=T(427) **Sept.** Jere. 29-30=(56)=T(441) **Oct**. Eze. 41-42=(46)=T(431) **Nov.** Acts 9-10=(91)=T(476) **Dec** Heb. 7-8=(41)=T(426s)

**Day 18** Book 4 Ps. 90-95=(87) Prov.18=(24) I Thess. 1-4=(61) Luke 10-12=(155)=T(327)

Ecclesiastes 9:16 "**Then said I,** (Solomon) **Wisdom is better than strength: nevertheless the <u>poor</u> man's**

**wisdom is despised, and his words are not heard.** (KJV)
James warns us about the poor

**Jan.** Gen. 35-36=(72) T=(388) **Feb.** Lev. 8-9=(60)=T(376)
**March** Deut. 9-10=(52)=T(366) **April** I Sam. 5-6=(34)=T(348)
**May** I Kings 11-12=(77)=T(391) **June** II Chr. 4-6=(78)=t(393)
**July** Job 10-12=(68)=T(381) **Aug.** Isa. 29-30=(57)=T(372)
**Sept**. Jere. 31-32=(84)=T(299) **Oct**. Eze. 43-44=(58)=T(373)
**Nov**. Acts 11-12=(55)=T(368) **Dec**. Heb. 9-10=(67)=T(382)

**Day19** Ps. 96-102=(84) Prov.19=(29) IThess.5 and II
Thess.1-3=(75) Luke 13-15=(102) =T(290)

Isaiah 9:16 "**For the leaders of this people** (What
people? v.12a (The syrians, before and the Philistines
behind) **cause them** (the Jews) **to err;** (blind leaders leading
the blind) **and they that are led of them are destroyed."**
(KJV) (To follow a vein or corrupt or unlearn people will
ruin you and themselves also) to "err" is the middle word
here. To err is not wrong, but to stay there is. My best
learning curve comes when I do err and confess it. But soon
get myself up and learn the lesson of why I fell in the first
place.

**Jan.** Gen. 37-38(66)=T(356) **Feb.** Lev. 10-
11=(67)=T(357) **March** Deut. 11-12=(64)=T(354) **April** I
Sam. 7-8=(39)=T(329) **May** I Kings 13-14=(65=)355)=T(395)
**June** II Chr 7-8=(40)=t(330) **July** Job 13-15=(85)=T(375)
**Aug**. Isa. 31-32=(29)=T(319) **Sept**. Jere. 33-34=(48)=T(338)
**Oct**. Eze. 45-46=(49)=T(339) **Nov**. Acts 13-14=(79)=T(369)
**Dec**. Heb. 11-13=(94)=T(384)

**Day 20** Ps.103-104=(57 Prov. 20=(30) I Tim.1-3=(51)
Lu. 16-18=(111)=T (249)

Jeremiah 9:16 "**I** (Jehovah God) **will scatter them**
(the Jewish people) **also among the heathen**, (the ungodly

nations around them) **whom neither they nor their fathers have known: and I will send a sword after them till I have consumed them."** (God will not spare His vengeance) "have" is the middle two words in this verse is "have know" and it shows possession and ownership. This is what God is showing the people of Israel, that they are not their own.

I Corinthians 6:19-20 **"What? know ye not that your body is the temple of the Holy Ghost which is in you, which ye have of God, and ye are not your own? v.20 For ye are bought with a price: therefore glorify God in your body, and in your spirit, which are God's."** (KJV)

**Jan**. Gen 39-40(46)=T(295) **Feb**. Lev. 12-13=(67) =T(316) **March** Deut. 13-14=(47)=T(296) **April** I Sam.9-10=(54) =T(303) **May** 1 Kings 15-16=(68)=T(317) **June 11** Chr. 9-10=(50)=t(299) **July** Job 16-18=(59) =T(308) **Aug**. Isa. 33-34=(41)=T(290) **Sept**. Jere. 35-36=(51)=T(300) **Oct**. Eze. 47-48 =(58)=T(307) **Nov**. Acts 15-16=T(81)=T(330) **Dec**. Rev. 1-2=(49)=T(298)

**Day 21** Ps. 105-106=(93) Prov. 21=(31) I Tim. 4-6=(62 Luke 19-21=(133)=T(319)

Daniel 9:16 **""O LORD** (Jehovah/Yahweh) **according to all thy righteousness,**(righteous Judgements) **I beseech thee, let thine anger and fury be turned away from thy city Jer/ USA/LEM, thy holy mountain: because for our sins, and for the iniquities of our fathers, Jer/USA/LEM and thy people are become a reproach to all that are about us."** (KJV) This verse has 51 words in it, one of my longest birthday verses.

**Jan**. Gen 41-42=(95)=T(414 **Feb**. Lev. 14-15=(90)=T(409) **March** Deut.15-16=(45)=T(364) **April** I Sam. 11-12=(40)=T(359) **May** I Kings 17-18=70=T(389) **June** II Chr.11-12=39=T(358) **July** Job 19-21=92=(411) **Aug**. Isa. 35-36=(32)=T(351) **Sept**.

Jere. 37-38=(49)=T(368) **Oct.** miss readings **Nov.** Acts 17-18=(62)=T(381) **Dec.** Rev. 3-4=(33)=T(352)

**Day 22** Book 5 Ps 107-109=(87) Prov. 22=(29) II Tim.1-4= (83) Luke 22-24=(180)= T (379)

Zechariah 9:16 "**And the Lord their God shall save them**" (Israel) **in that day as the flock of his people: for they shall be as the stones of a crown, lifted up as an ensign** (a flag amount the people) **upon His land."** (KJV) (God's land, Psalm 24:1a **the earth and the fulness thereof**)

**Jan.** Gen. 43-44=(68) =T(447) **Feb.** Lev. 16-17=(50)=T(429) **March** Deut.17-18=(42)=T(421) **April** I Sam. 13-14=(75)=T(454) **May** I kings 19-20=(64)=T(443) **June** II Chron.13-14=(37)=t(416) **July** Job 22-24=(72)=T(451) **Aug.** Isa. 37-38=(60)=T(439) **Sept.** Jere. 39-40=(34)=T(413) **Oct.** miss readings **Nov.** Acts 19-20=(79)=T(458) **Dec.** Rev. 5-6=(31)=T(410)

**Day 23** Ps. 110-115=(62) Prov. 23=(35) Titus 1-3 & Phil 1=(71) John 1-3=(112)=T (280)

Matthews 9:16 "**No man putteth a piece of new cloth unto an old garment, for that which is put in to fill it up taketh from the garment, and the rent is made worse."** (KJV)

**Jan.** Gen. 45-46=(62)=T(342) **Feb.** Lev. 18-19=(67)=T(347) **March** Deut..19-20=(41)=T(321) **April** I Sam. 15-16=(58)=T(338) **May** I Kings 21-22=(82)=T(362) **June** II Chr.15-16=(33)=t(313) **July** Job 25-27=(43)=T(323) **Aug.** Isa. 39-40=(39)=T(319) **Sept.** Jere. 41-42=(40)=T(320) **Oct.** Dan.1-3=(100)=T(380) **Nov.** Acts 21-22=(70)=T(350) **Dec.** Rev. 7-8=(30)=T(310)

**Day 24** Ps. 116-118=(50) Prov. 24=(34) James 1-5=(108) John 4-6=(172)= T(364)

Mark 9:16 "**And He** (Jesus) **asked the <u>scribes, What</u> question you with them?**" (KJV)

**Jan.** Gen. 47-48=(53) =T(417) **Feb.** Lev. 20-21=(51)=T(415) March Deut. 21-22=(53)=T(417) **April** I Sam. 17-18=(88)=T(452) **May** II Kings 1-3=(70)=T(434) **June** II Chr. 17-18=(53)=t(417) **July** Job 28-30=(84)=T.(448) **Aug.** Isa. 41-42=(54)=T(418) **Sept.** Jere. 43-44=(43)=T(407) **Oct.** Dan. 4-6=(96)=T(460) **Nov.** Acts 23-24=(62)=T(426) **Dec.** Rev. 9-10=(32)=T(396)

**Day 25** Ps.119: 1-88=(88) Prov. 25=(28) I Peter 1-2=(50) John 7-9=(153)= T (319)

Luke 9:16 "**Then He** (Jesus) **took the five loaves and the two fishes, and looking up to heaven, He blessed them and brake, and gave to the disciples to set (serve) before the multitude.**" (KJV) This is a 30 word verse. The middle two words are "heaven/He" this is it, heaven to gain and Jesus, God) to thank for your salvation.

**Jan.** Gen. 49-50 (59)=T (379) **Feb.** Lev. 22-23=(78)=T(397) **March** Deut. 23-24=(47)=T(366) **April** I Sam 19-20=(66)=T(385) **May** II Kings 4-6=(104)=T(423) **June** II Chr. 19-20=(48)=t(367) **July** Job 31-33=(95)=T(414) **Aug.** Isa. 43-44=(56)=T(375) **Sept** Jere. 45-46=(33)=T(352) Oct. Dan. 7-9=(82)=T(411) **Nov.** Acts 25-26=(59)=T(378) **Dec.** Rev. 11-12=(36)=T(355)

**Day 26** Ps 119:89-176=(88)-Prov. 26=(28)=T(347) I Peter 3-5=(55) John 10-12=(149)=T (320)

John 9:16 "**Therefore said some of the Pharisees, This man is not of God, because He keepeth not the sabbath <u>day</u>. Others said, How can a man that is a sinner do such miracles?** (now these people at the last are making a lot of sense) **And there was a division among them**" (KJV) with Christ Jesus there will always be a division.

Thirty nine words in this verse, one of my longer birthday verses. The middle word is "day" today if you hear the voice of God, harden not your hearts.

**Jan.** Ex. 1-3=(69)=T(389) **Feb.** Lev. 24-25=(78)=T(398) **March** Deut. 25-26=(38)=T(358) **April** I Sam. 21-22=(32)=T(452) **May** II Kings 7-8=(49)=T(369) **June** II Chr. 21-22=(32)=t(352) **July** Job 34-36=(86)=T(406) **Aug**. Isa. 45-46=(38)=T(358) **Sept.** Jere. 47-48=(54)=T(347) **Oct.** Dan. 10-12=(79)=T(399) **Nov**. Acts 27-28=(75)=T(395) **Dec.** Rev. 13-14=(38)=T(358)

**Day 27** Ps. 120-131=(77) Prov. 27=(27) II Peter 1-3=(61) John 13-14=(69)=T=(234)

Romans 9:16 "**So then it is not of him that willeth, <u>nor of</u> him that runneth, but of God that showeth mercy.**" (KJV) Get our eyes off of self and look to the Lord who has great grace and mercy.

"So then" in verse 16 is referring to verse 15 "**For He (Jesus) saith to Moses, I will have mercy on whom I will have mercy, and I will have compassion on whom I will have compassion**" (KJV)

**Jan.** Ex. 4-5 (54) =T (288) **Feb.** Lev. 26-27=(80)= T(314 **March** Deut. 27-28=(94)=T(328) **April** I Sam. 23-24=(51)=T(285) **May** II Kings 9-10=(73)= T(307) **June** II Chr. 23-24= (48)=t282) **July** Job 37-39=(95)=T(329) **Aug**. Isa. 47-48=(37)=T(271) **Sept.** Jere. 49-50=(85)= T(319 **Oct.** Hosea 1-3= (39)=T(273) **Nov.** Rom. 1-3=(92)=T(326) **Dec.** Rev. 15-16=(29)=T(263)

**Day 28** Ps. 132-137=(80) Prov. 28=(28) I John 1-3=(63) John 15-16=(60) = T(231)

Acts 9:16 "**For I** (Jesus) **will shew him** (Saul, later Paul) **how great <u>things</u> he** (Saul) **must suffer for my name's**

**sake.**" (KJV) Jesus was talking to Ananias, a follower of Christ, about Saul the new convert

**Jan.** Ex. 6-7 (55)= T(286) **Feb.** Nu. 1-3=(139)=T(370) **March** Deut. 29-30(49)=T(280) **April** I Sam. 25-26=(69) =T(300) **May** II Kings 11-12=(42)=T(273) **June** II Chr.25-27=(60)=T(291) **July** Job 40-42=(75)=T(306) **Aug.** Isa. 49-50=(37)=T(268) **Sept.** Jere. 51-52=(98)=T(329) **Oct.** Hosea 4-6=(45)=T(276) **Nov..** Rom. 4-6=(69)=T(300) **Dec.** Rev. 17-18=(42)=T(273)

**Day 29** Ps.138-144=(89) Prov. 29=(27) I John 4-5=(42) John. 17-19=(108)= T(266)

I Corinthians 9:16 "**For though I preach the gospel. I have nothing to glory of: for necessity** (compelling) **is laid upon me; yea woe** (warning signs) **is unto me, if I preach not the gospel** (KJV)

**Jan.** Ex.8-10 =(96) = T (362) **Feb.** Nu. 4-6=(107)=T(373) **March** Deut. 31-32=(82)=T(348) **April** I Sam. 27-28=(37)=T(303) **May** II Kings 13-14=(54)=T(320) **June** II Chr. 28-30=(90)=t(356) **July** Ecc.1-3=(66)=T(332) **Aug**. Isa. 51-52=(38)=T(304) **Sept.** Eze. 1-3=(65)=T(331) **Oct.** Hosea 7-9=(47)=T(313) **Nov**. Rom 7-8=(64)=T(330) **Dec.** Rev. 19-20=(36)=T(302)

**Day 30** Ps. 145-150=(80) Prov. 30=(33) II&III John & Jude=(52) John 20-21=(56)= T (221)

Hebrews 9:16 "**For where a testament is, there must also of necessity be the death of the testator.**" KJV There are 16 words in this verse and the two middle words are "also of" Jesus paid the ultimate price for us. Eugene Peterson's book the message has this verse this way. "**His** (Jesus) **death marked the transition from the old plan** (the law) **to the new one.**" MSG (Grace age) God is talking to Ananais the prophet in this verse, In order to have one, you have the other, a testament and the Testor.(Jesus)

**Jan.** Ex. 11-12 =(61) =T (282) **Feb.** Nu. 7-9=138=T(359) **March** Deut. 33-34=(41)=T(262) I **April** I Sam. 29-31=(55)=(276) **May** II Kings 15-16=(58)=T(277) **June** II Chr. 31-33=(79)=t(300) **July** Ecc. 4-6=(48)=T(269) **Aug.** Isa.53-54=(29)=T(250) **Sept.** Eze. 4-6=(48)=T(276 **Oct.** Hosea 10-12=(41)=T(262) **Nov.** Rom 9-10=(54)=T(275) **Dec.** Rev. 21-22=(48)=T(269)

**Day 31** Prov. 31=(31) **A good women,** Genesis 3=(24) John 3=(36) **salvation** Matt.5-7=(111) **Jesus' teachings** I Corinthians 13=(13) **Agobe love** Ecclesiastes 3=(22) **Seasons of time,** we have **times** and **seasons** in one's life. Psalm 1=(6) **Blessed** Psalm 23=(6) **the shepherd's psalm,** Psalm 51=(19) **the confessing psalm,** Psalm 150=(6) **Peace Psalm,** Isaiah 53=(12) **Suffering on the cross foretold,** Eph. 6=(24) **the armour of God,** James 3=(18) **the tongue chapter** T(328) and any other verses that you are behind on or just like to read.

My birthday verse for today is:

Revelations 9:16 "**And the number of the army of the horsemen were <u>two</u> hundred thousand thousand: (200,000,000) and I heard the number of them**" There are 21 words in this verse and the middle number is "two" their verse deals with numbers. This verse signifies that there are 200,000,000, yes 200 Million soldiers.

If this is done correctly, you have read: The gospels 12 times per year, The Psalm 12 times, Proverbs 12 times

The 27 short books of 6 chapters and under 12 times

10 in the OT and 17 in the NT.

The readings of the month that has 31 days in them,

7 more times =19 times, 12 and 7

There 7 Months w/31 days, 4 months w/30 days and 1 month w/ 28 days and every 3 years 29 days, with this month double up on days 27 and 28

The remainder bible of 33 books, one time per year

My birthday verse, 916 verses from the beginning is Genesis chapter 31:42 "**Except the God of my father, the God of Abraham, and the fear of Issac, had been with me, surely thou hadst sent me away not empty. God hath seen mine affliction and the labour of my hands and rebuked thee yesterday night.**" (KJV) Jacob was talking and referring to Laban, his father-in-law.

Jacob was angry with his father-in-law Laban, Jacob gives God the credit for saving his life and his substance. We are in a crooked and perverse generation. Evil is lucking all around us. Thank God for His protection.

There are 33 books that have 9 hundred and sixteen verses in them.

Philippians 2:15c "**...in the midst of a crooked and perverse nation, among whom you shine as lights in this world.** The darker the night, brighter is our Spiritual light. This light is our faith. Romans 10:17 "**So faith cometh by hearing, and hearing by the word of God.**" (KJV)

Psalm 119:11 "**Thy word has I hid in mind heart, that I might not sin against thee.**" (Jesus Christ)(KJV emphasis added)

The study of God's word is essential to spiritual growth.

I am amazed at the daily comparisons of the word in the scriptures that I read. Let me give you an example: Day one you have the blessings in Psalms, in Proverbs you have the understanding of a proverb and the blessings in Ruth and her mother-in-law with her baby (Obed) in Matthew you see the blessings of Mary giving birth to our Savior, many, many the similarities running through the book that you read once per year. Only God can do this.

There are 40 different writers, in different times, who could orchestrate such a masterpiece. II Peter 1:21 "**For the prophecy came not in old time by the will of men: but holy men of God spake as they were moved by the Holy Ghost.**" (Spirit) (KJV, emphasis added)

John 5:39 "**Search the scriptures, for in them** (the word, the bible) **you think you have eternal life: and they** (the word) **are they** (the word) **which testify of me** (Jesus) (KJV, emphasis added)

I like to add my birthday verses. In doing so, I personalize the Bible to me. I like to write, mark up any books that I read, so I can see myself in my books. I have a separate paper on my birthday verse. I was born on September 16, Sept being the ninth month, and the 16$^{th}$ day of the month. There are 31 books with 9:16 in them, Genesis 9:16, Psalms 9:16, Matthew 9:16 and so on. Being there are 31 days in 7 of the months, I like to read one verse per day of that month. What are your birthday verses? If you were born on January 1-6, you would have 66 birthday verses. After January 6$^{th}$ you not more then 65 birthday verses If you were born on 12:31, you have 15 birthday verses.

May the Lord keep you by His word. May you personalize the bible just as I did. Let it be part of your life too.

Printed in the United States
by Baker & Taylor Publisher Services